故園畫憶

庚寅中秋
韓磬池題

《故园画忆系列》编委会

名誉主任： 韩启德

主　　任： 邵　鸿

委　　员：（按姓氏笔画为序）

万　捷	王秋桂	方李莉	叶培贵
刘魁立	况　晗	严绍璗	吴为山
范贻光	范　芳	孟　白	邵　鸿
岳庆平	郑培凯	唐晓峰	曹兵武

故园画忆系列
MEMORY OF THE OLD
HOME IN SKETCHES

袁州记忆
Memory of Yuanzhou

严兴河　绘画　撰文
Sketches & Notes by Yan Xinghe

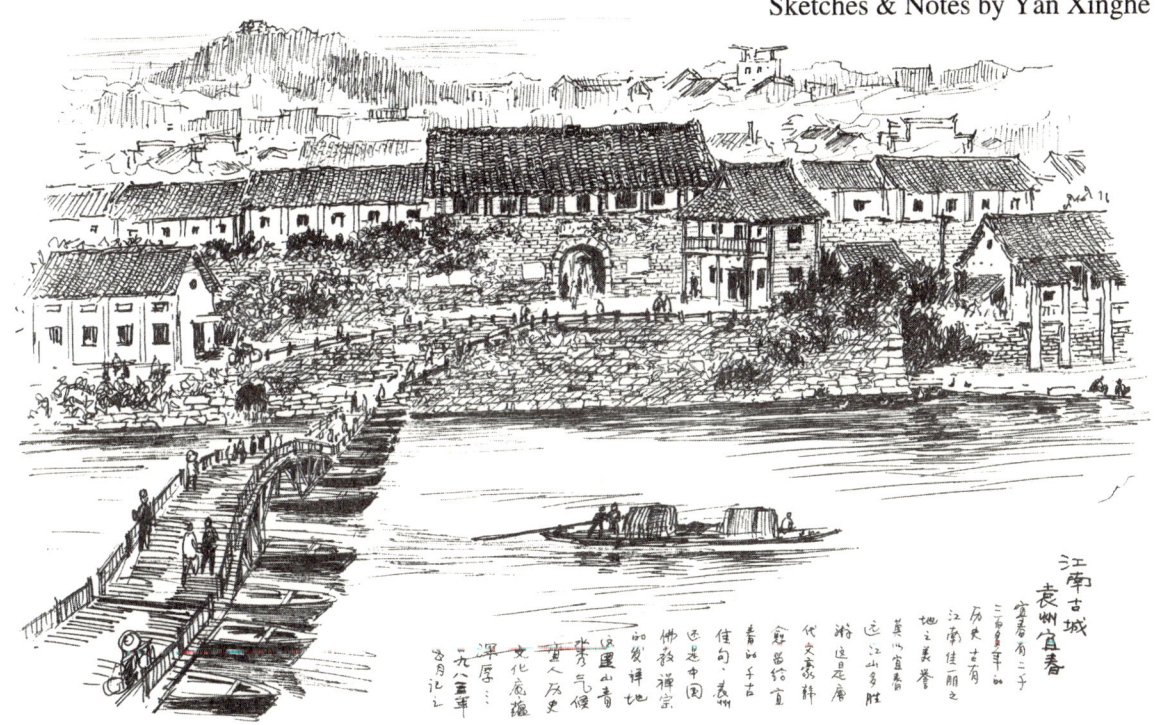

学苑出版社
ACADEMY PRESS

图书在版编目（CIP）数据

袁州记忆 / 严兴河绘画、撰文. — 北京：学苑出版社，2015.11
（故园画忆系列）
ISBN 978-7-5077-4910-6

Ⅰ.①袁… Ⅱ.①严… Ⅲ.①钢笔画—作品集—中国—现代②宜春市—概况
Ⅳ.①J224②K925.63

中国版本图书馆CIP数据核字（2015）第259922号

出 版 人：	孟　白
责任编辑：	洪文雄　周　鼎
出版发行：	学苑出版社
社　　址：	北京市丰台区南方庄2号院1号楼
邮政编码：	100079
网　　址：	www.book001.com
电子信箱：	xueyuan@public.bta.net.cn
联系电话：	010-67601101（营销部）、67603091（总编室）
经　　销：	全国新华书店
印 刷 厂：	三河市灵山红旗印刷厂
开本尺寸：	889×1194　1/24
印　　张：	6.25
字　　数：	150千字
图　　幅：	127幅
版　　次：	2015年11月北京第1版
印　　次：	2015年11月北京第1次印刷
定　　价：	45.00元

目　录

序　　　　　　　　　　　　　　毛静

人文遗迹

南池涌珠	3
宜春台	4
高安古大观楼	5
古保安门	6
鼓楼旧景	7
鼓楼广场	8
仰山栖隐禅寺	9
难禅阁	10
化成寺	11
显应禅寺	12
慈化寺	13
杨岐普通寺	14
万佛庙	15
普利禅寺	16
报恩寺旧址	17
南禅塔	18
文笔峰古塔	19
万载文明塔	20
雷火塔	21
昌山庙	22
宜丰岳王庙	23
宜春文庙·大成殿（一）	24
宜春文庙·大成殿（二）	25
宜春文昌宫	26
宜春化成寺	27
昌黎书院	28
状元洲读书堂（一）	29
状元洲读书堂（二）	30
苏家古祠	31
竹坡公祠	32
毓庆堂	33
昌黎阁	34
老竹山的庐江堂	35
朱氏节孝牌坊	36
袁京墓	37
古城浮桥	38
金鸡桥	39
高安浮桥（一）	40
高安浮桥（二）	41
上高浮桥	42
宜春砥柱桥	43

鸣水桥	44
升瀛桥	45
大埠村石桥	46
双 桥	47
永宁桥老街	48
潭山老街（一）	49
潭山老街（二）	50
潭山老屋	51
昌黎巷	52
下浦老街	53
王子巷	54
泉井头老巷	55
潮溪村	56
新昌镇	57
易家老屋	58
锦江河边老屋	59
袁州老屋	60
高安石脑老屋	61
废弃的水车屋	62
化成岩下的农舍（一）	63
化成岩下的农舍（二）	64
滩下路的老屋	65
凤凰山下居民区	66
东城巷居民区	67
三眼古井	68
七眼古井	69
宜春耶稣堂	70

安源煤矿·总平巷	71
袁州会议旧址	72
铜鼓人民英雄碑	73
玻璃厂的老烟囱	74

自然风光

铜鼓石	77
上高锦江河边	78
仰山·千年古杏	79
仰山·梯田	80
明月山·小景	81
明月山·竹林月影	82
明月山·云谷飞瀑	83
洪江山林小景	84
状元洲旧景	85
筒车悠悠	86
袁河岸边小景	87
市郊边山路小景	88

民风民俗

三角班	91
三星鼓乐	92
万载傩舞	93
春锣艺人	94
舞龙队	95
脱胎漆器	96
手工夏布	97

松花皮蛋厂	98		乐在其中	116
乡村谷酒	99		大坪巷的早点摊	117
车葫芦工艺	100		缝补小摊位	118
弹棉工艺	101		温汤泡脚广场	119
水豆腐（一）	102		温汤古井	120
水豆腐（二）	103		茶　室	121
烟花鞭炮	104		理发匠人	122
清明祭祖	105		修理人力车	123
庙会集市	106		修伞者	124
街头陶瓷品	107		磨刀艺人	125
杂品市场	108		工棚一角	126
竹木杂品	109		鸭　苗	127
杂货店	110		屋前房后种瓜种豆	128
宜春汉春祥骑楼杂货店	111		城南郊外的菜地	129
称　店	112		滩下路的菜地	130
春台菜市场	113		西瓜上市	131
殷家蔬果市场	114		油茶林场的农户	132
箭道市场	115		九旬老母亲	133

后　记

Contents

Preface	Maojing

Cultural Relics

Pearl Springs in Nanchi	3
Yichun Terrace	4
Grand View Tower of in Gao'an City	5
Bao'an Gate	6
Old Drum Tower	7
Drum Tower Square	8
Qiyin Temple in Yangshan Mountain	9
Nanchan Hall	10
Huacheng Temple	11
Xianying Temple	12
Cihua Temple	13
Putong Temple in Yangqi	14
Wanfo Temple	15
Puli Temple	16
Bao'en Temple	17
Nanchan Pagoda	18
Tower on Mount Wenbi	19
Wenming Tower in Wanzai	20
Leihuo Tower	21
Changshan Temple	22
Yuewang Temple in Yifeng	23
Confucius Temple in Yichun, Dacheng Hall (1)	24
Wenmiao Temple of Yichun • Dacheng Hall (2)	25
Wenchang Palace in Yichun	26
Huacheng Temple in Yichun	27
Changli Academy	28
Zhuangyuan Islet Study (1)	29
Zhuangyuan Islet Study (2)	30
Clan Hall of the Su's Family	31
Zhupo Clan Hall	32
Yuqing Hall	33
Changli Building	34
Lujiang Hall on Laozhu Mountain	35
Xia Memorial Arch	36
Tomb of Yuan Jing	37
Floating Bridge in the Ancient Town	38
Jinji Bridge	39
Gao'an Floating Bridge (1)	40
Gao'an Floating Bridge (2)	41
Shanggao Floating Bridge	42
Dizhu Bridge of Yichun	43
Mingshui Bridge	44
Shengying Bridge	45
Stone Bridge in Dabu Village	46
Double Bridge	47

Yongning Bridge Street	48
Tanshan Street (1)	49
Tanshan Street (2)	50
Houses in Tanshan	51
Changli Lane	52
Xiapu Street	53
Prince Lane	54
Quanjingtou Lane	55
Chaoxi Village	56
Xinchang Town	57
Yi Clan Houses	58
Houses at Jingjiang River	59
House in Yuanzhou	60
House in Shinao of Gaoan	61
Waterwheel Houses	62
Cottages under Huacheng Cliff (1)	63
Cottages under Huacheng Cliff (2)	64
Houses on Tanxia Road	65
Community at the foot of Phoenix Mountain	66
Dongchengxiang Community	67
Sanyan Well	68
Seven-Outlet Well	69
Chapel in Yichun	70
Anyuan Coal Mine - Zongping Lane	71

Site of the Yuanzhou Conference	72
Monument to the People's Heroes in Tonggu	73
Weichang Glass Factory Chimneys	74

Natural Landscape

Tonggu Stone	77
Jinjiang Riverbanks, Shanggao County	78
Yanshan Mountain• Apricots	79
Yanshan Mountain terrace fields	80
Mingyue Mountain Scenic Location	81
Mingyue Mountain - Bamboo Shadow in Moonlight	82
Mingyue Mountain - Yungu Falls	83
Hongjiang Forest Site in Hongjiang Town	84
Zhuangyuan Islet Site	85
Waterwheels	86
Sight at Yuanhe River	87
Suburban Mountain Path Site	88

Folk Customs

Sanjiaoban Opera	91
Sanxing Drum Music	92
Wanzai Nuo Dance	93
Artists Performing Spring Gong	94
Dragon-Dance Team	95

Baseless Lacquer ware	96		Jiandao Market	115
Handmade Xia Cloth	97		Enjoying Life	116
Preserved-Egg Workshop	98		Breakfast Stalls in Daping Lane	117
Village-Made Rice Wine	99		Stalls for Sewing and Mending	118
Che Gourd Handicraft	100		Foot-Spa Square, Wentang Town	119
Cotton Fluffing Technique	101		Wentang Town Well	120
Soft Bean Curd (1)	102		Tea Room	121
Soft Bean Curd (2)	103		Barber	122
Fireworks and Firecrackers	104		Repairing Rickshaws	123
Worship Ritual for Ancestral Tomb-Sweeping Day	105		Craftsman Repairing Umbrellas	124
Temple Fair	106		Craftsman Sharpening Knives	125
Ceramic Works in Street	107		A Bunkhouse Corner	126
Sundry Goods Market	108		Ducklings	127
Sundry Products of Bamboo and Wood	109		House Vegetable Gardens	128
Groceries	110		A Southern Suburb Vegetable Field	129
Arcade Grocery in Hanchunxiang, Yichun	111		Vegetable Field on Tanxia Road	130
Weight Measurement Scales (Steelyards) Store	112		Watermelons Ready for Sale	131
Vegetable Market in Chuntai Park	113		Farmers in a Camellia Farm	132
Yin Clan Vegetable and Fruit Market	114		My Mother in Her 90s	133

Later on

序

如果一座城市没有一批为之守望的文学家或艺术家,这座城市也许是不幸的;所幸袁州就有不少与之长相厮守的守望者,严兴河老师就是其中一位。

知道严兴河先生,是从吴静男老师送给我的《西赣文化》中有过疏浅的了解。每期的杂志都会配发一批严老师的剪纸或者速写,让我感觉到,这是一位用心表现宜春风景与民俗的画家。

其实严老师是分宜人,从"介子堂"的堂号可以知道,他还是明代严嵩的族裔。由于行政区划的变化,宋代从宜春分出去的"分宜"现在成为新余市的属县,但是,历史所形成的文化惯性却不会随之割断。直到现在,分宜和萍乡的人都有浓重的袁州情结,毕竟"一府四县"的时间长达一千多年。"吴头楚尾"的赣西地区有着共有的文化基因,共同的文化记忆和历史认同,使"一府四县"仍是一个隐然存在的地域空间。

严老师生于分宜,却在这里生活了四十年。他自宜春师专毕业分配到宜春电影公司工作以后,就再也没有离开过这里。由于学的是美术,他的艺术触角自然而然地延伸到了相关门类,于是摄影、书法、剪纸、版画、速写等都成为严老师常用的艺术表现手法。唯一不变的是他创作题材,他用自己的画笔、刀剪或镜头,忠实记录着这个城市的变化。可以说,他浓重的乡土情结,就深深渗透在他的作品里。发自内心的人文关怀,让他与袁州相依相守,不离不弃。面对不断解构与重建的城市格局、不断嬗变与进化的风土与人情,严老师用心在记录着这座城市微妙的变化。在时光的雕琢之中,自己也年华老去,使他的守望多少带着一丝悲壮的色彩;但是,艺术家的心灵永远年轻,他们内心的快乐,不是常人所能洞察,我们只有从他们历久弥健的笔墨和刀锋中,能感觉到他们旺盛的创作激情和源源不断的灵感,犹如明月山的飞瀑和温汤的沸泉。

2015年元月,笔者偶有机会从高校下派到地方挂职。到袁州以后,就在思考一个问题,如何发掘利用一些文字和图像，更真实地表现这个地方的历史和文化？20世纪70年代以来，本地的风景名胜、风土人情等方面的资料，有没有人曾经记录过它们的沧桑变迁？这时，吴静男老师向我推荐了严兴河先生。严先生为人谦谨，给人以诚恳而真实的印象，仿佛读他艺术作品，就能读懂他的为人，使我感觉，这是一位德艺双馨的好师长，于是我感到用"严老师"来称呼他是更为正确的。在接下来的时间里，我和严老师既有用分宜话对话的趣事，也有一起在草莽中寻震山卢肇题刻、在菜地里访文笔塔遗址、在朝阳路翻觅唐宋李渠遗迹和在居民区里找七眼井的经历。特别是严老师痛心疾首地讲述1999年左右政府大拆宋代古城墙的举措，真是让人感到切肤之痛。他独自保护秀江门匾，十年后捐献给宜春市城市规划展览馆的义举，更是令我更是肃然起敬。

几个月来，在严老师仅可容膝旋踵的工作室，我们在晴窗雨槛前有过多次愉快的交谈，也曾有幸看到了他收藏的古砖、雕刻的版画、剪刻的剪纸、拍摄的老照片以及其他作品。总之，我总觉得严老师是一位讷于言而敏于行的艺术家，严谨、勤奋且谦虚，从作品中可以探知他对艺术的追求和与世无争的恬淡心境。当我提出将他四十年间所画的宜春题材速写集中出版时，严老师显得略有些迟疑。我知道他不是对自己作品不自信，而是现在出版这些老皇历、旧题材多少显得有些"不合时宜"，他顾虑的是好的作品有没有人欣赏。但是我认为，时下的确有人会数典忘祖，会"茫然走在路上，却忘了自己为什么而出发"，文艺界、学术界所表现出来焦虑与狂躁，甚至放浪形骸的情绪弥漫整个社会，无不引起有识之士的深深忧虑。我们出版这些寻找故园的图书，不是为悦时媚世，而更多地是在寻找历史年轮中刻下的痕迹，通过或浓或淡的笔触，带我们回到回不去的童年和故园，何尝不是一种"精神抵达"？

现在，我们从选出的这百余幅速写作品中，可以一窥近半个世纪来袁州历史变迁的记忆片断。在严老师的画笔下，展现了一幅幅升斗小民日常生活的精细画面。有小溪边咿咿呀呀的水车，有蕉园边干打垒的土坯房，有市场上补伞打铁的匠人，也有游走在寻常巷陌的江湖郎中。总之，一百多幅画是半个世纪以来袁州百姓的起居小景，举手投足都是扑面而来的生活气息。我把它推荐给学苑出版社的《故园画忆》系列丛书，希望能作为体现江西本土文化特色的一枚拼图，共同组成故园记忆的宏丽画卷。

乙未菊月，剑川毛静撰于袁州郡斋震山堂

Preface

I live in Yichun City. In January 2005, I was wondering how to find the words and images to showcase the history and culture of the city in a more vivid manner and whether there were any records of the changes of the scenery and customs of this city since the 1970's in particular. During that time someone introduced to me Mr. Yan Xinghe, a modest, sincere gentleman. His works are a real depiction of his personality. Coming from Fenyi County of Yuanzhou City, Yan clearly understood the cultural identity of Yichun. Moreover, Yan Song, one of his ancestors and a grand secretary in during the Ming Dynasty (1368-1644), was an important figure of that culture.

I have had happy conversations with Mr. Yan in his studio several times during these past months, in which I, and our readers, can feel his affection for the pursuit of arts and his indifference to fame and fortune. When I expressed my hope to publish his sketches of Yichun he made during the past four decades, he was somewhat hesitant. I was aware that it was not because he was not confident in his works, but because he thought these old works and topics were not popular any more. However, I believe that publishing these sketches, for the purpose of portraying the old town, is about depicting its history through our own humble brushes and refreshing our memories of our childhood and hometown.

Now, from over one hundred sketches, we can get a glimpse of the historical changes in Yichun over the past half-decade. Yan, through his brushes, demonstrates in detail ordinary people and things in daily life, like the chattering waterwheels on rivers, clay houses in construction beside a banana grove, craftsmen mending umbrellas and forging iron on the streets, folk doctors wandering the streets, etc. I recommend this collection to the Academy Press as a part of the Memory of the Old Home in Sketches Series, hoping that it will contribute to the depiction of the local features of Jiangxi Province, together with other books forming a touching album of our hometowns.

Mao Jing
At Jun Mansion, Yuanzhou City
September 2015

人文遗迹
Cultural Relics

> 南池涌珠

　　宜春因泉而得名，此地有泉"莹碧如春，饮之宜人"曰宜春泉。城南池泉如涌，泉带气泡如珠，故曰"南池涌珠"，此为宜春城古八景之一旧址。图为1988年的景象。

Pearl Springs in Nanchi

Yichun City is famous for its natural springs, many of which are in the southern part of the city. As they give up bubbles like shining pearls, they got the name Pearl Springs. It is among the Eight Historic Sites in Yichun City. This is a depiction of the site in 1988.

宜春台

位于袁州区中山中路，古袁州治所的宜春城中制高点，海拔130.4米。汉武帝元光六年（前129年）宜春侯刘成于城中设五台，其中最胜者为宜春台，故有"高出袁城百万家，巍峨楼殿锁烟霞"之美景，是宜春古八景之首。

Yichun Terrace

Located on Middle Zhongshan Road in Yuanzhou District, the terrace is 130.4 meters high -- the highest point in the city. It used to be the official premises of ancient Yuanzhou. In 129 BC, Liu Cheng, the head of Yichun built five terraces, among which Yichun Terrace is the most magnificent and renowned as the most important among the Eight Historic Sites in Yichun.

高安古大观楼

原名锦水奇观楼，位于高安市锦江北岸，始建于宋元丰年间（1078～1085年），北宋文豪苏辙留有诗句"苍然暮色映楼台，江市游人夜未回"，清嘉庆二十年（1815年）再次重建后，取范仲淹《岳阳楼记》"……岳阳楼之大观也"之意改名为大观楼。这幅画作完成于1979年。

Grand View Tower of in Gao'an City

Located on the north bank of Jingjiang River in Gao'an City, it was formerly referred to as Jingshui Viewing Tower. Originally built between 1078 and 1085, it was rebuilt in 1815. Again destroyed by war, it was rebuilt and given its present name. This painting was finished in 1979.

古保安门

位于袁州区新坊乡南边，宜春至安福的边关古驿道，城门牌楼"保安门"为清咸丰年间（1850～1861年）建造，门长27.3米，高5米，深4.68米，至今保存尚好。

Bao'an Gate

With Xinfang Town of Yuanzhou District to its north, the gate was on an ancient courier route from Yichun City to Anfu City. First built from 1850 and 1861, the gate is 27.3 meters long, 5 meters high and 4.68 meters wide. It has been very well preserved.

鼓楼旧景

位于袁州区鼓楼步行商业街中央,又名袁州谯楼,始建于南唐保大二年(944年),后南宋嘉定十二年(1219年)知州滕强恕制铀壶、漏箭、影表、水海、定南针、更筹、铁板等器具,设阴阳生轮值、候筹报时,将其建成了集测时、守时、授时于一体的天文台。明清两代多次重修,现为清末建筑。这是鼓楼维修前的旧景,速写于2003年4月。

Old Drum Tower

Located in the middle of Drum-Tower Street in Yuanzhou District, it is also known as Qiaolou Tower of Yuanzhou. First built in 944, it was rebuilt as an observatory in 1219 by Teng Qiangshu, a local administrator. Revamped several times during the Ming (1368-1644) and Qing (1644-1911) Dynasties, the existing part was rebuilt in the late Qing Dynasty. This painting, finished in April, 2003, depicts the tower before the latest reconstruction.

鼓楼广场

20世纪80年代后,过全面修复,恢复明清格调的宜春鼓楼和一座颇具宜春地方特色的天文广场,正式向市民开放,其古典韵味与现代气息、传统风貌与开放意识和谐地交织在一起,延续着底蕴深厚的宜春文脉。现为城内最著名文化景观之一。

Drum Tower Square

After reconstruction during the 1980s, Drum Tower Square still has Ming (1368-1644) and Qing (1644-1911) Dynasties features including an astronomical square with local characteristics. It has been open to the public since then and is one of the city's most famous cultural sites.

仰山栖隐禅寺

位于袁州区老城南23千米的明月山集云峰下,由开山祖师慧寂禅师始建于唐会昌五年(845年),宋太平兴国年间(976~984年),奉敕改名为"太平兴国寺",元朝大德七年(1303年)年至20世纪60年代多次毁于火灾,本世纪初重建该寺。为禅宗五家之一的沩仰宗祖庭。

Qiyin Temple in Yangshan Mountain

Located behind Mount Jiyun of the Mingyue Mountain Range, 23 kilometers south to the old town of Yuanzhou, it was founded in 845 by Monk Huiji and later got the name Taipingxingguo Temple. Destroyed by fire, it was rebuilt at the beginning of this century. It is a Buddhist Zuting (a temple where monks of a Buddhist Sect live, teach and are buried after death) of the Weiyang Sect, one of five Zen Buddhist sects.

难禅阁

位于袁州区鼓楼步行街，始建于北宋绍圣年间（1094～1097年），是时任袁州府司理李仲元参禅修道之所。后来，国才正儒黄庭坚题匾并撰《难禅阁铭》。阁楼呈正方形，庑殿顶，抬梁式木结构架建筑，虽历经千年，但主体结构仍保存完好。

Nanchan Hall
Located in Drum Tower Street in Yuanzhou District, this square building was first built between 1094 and 1097 as a place to practice Buddhism for Li Zhongyuan, an official in charge of litigation in Yuanzhou. Its main part remains intact even after nearly a thousand years.

化成寺

  位于袁州区西郊秀江河北岸化成岩森林公园内，始建于唐初，原为上、下两寺，上岩为开化院，下岩为惠明院。唐朝宰相李德裕贬至宜春，在此隐读，名声大增，此地为宜春古八景之一的"化成晚钟"，寺建历史有1200多年。清康熙年间，袁州知府李芳春题额"赞化裁成"，方改今名。

Huacheng Temple

Built in Huachengyan Forest Park on the north bank of Xiujiang River, which is in the western suburb of Yuanzhou District during the early Tang Dynasty (618-907), it became famous when Li Deyu, then Prime Minister, was banished to Yichun and devoted himself to studying. Evening Bell in Huacheng, one of the Eight Historic Sites of Yichun, is in this 1200 temple.

显应禅寺

　　为于明月山温泉风景名胜区境内的温汤镇田心村。寺院占地30亩,分为新寺与旧庙两部分。显应禅寺前身为始建于清康熙年间(1662~1722年)的"左将军庙",道光十六年(1836年)重建,改额曰"显应古庙"。2001年7月,聘请圣愿法师为住持,启动道场修复工程。2008年建成,现名为显应禅寺。

Xianying Temple
Originally built in Tianxin Village, Wentang Town in the Spring Scenic Area of Mingyue Mountain between 1622 and 1722 as the Temple of General Zuo, it is divided into an old and a new yards which together cover 30 mu of land. In 1836 it was rebuilt and given its current name.

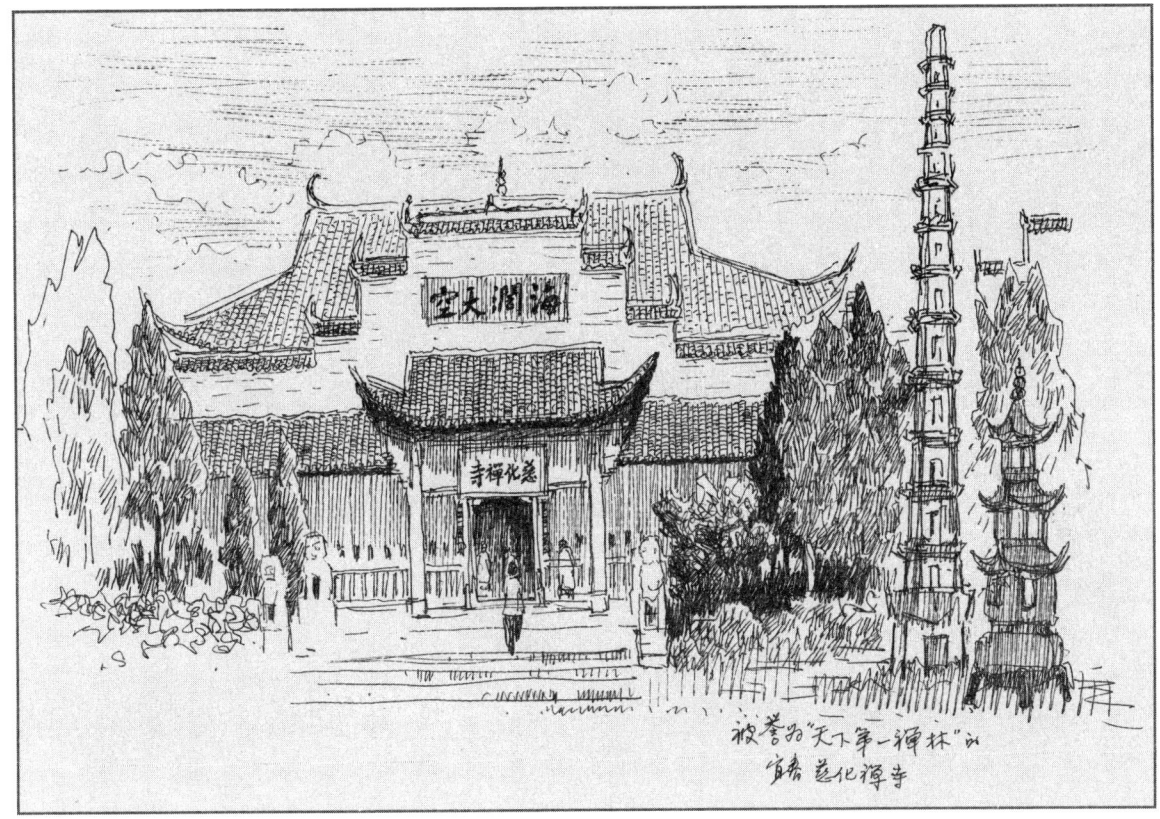

慈化寺

位于袁州区慈化镇南泉山，始建于南宋乾道二年（1166年），开山祖师为普庵禅师。历经宋、元、明、清四朝，已经有840多年历史，多次得到皇帝诏封御题，慈化寺鼎盛之时建有10座殿堂，共2000多间房屋，占地6万多平方米，纳僧千名。

Cihua Temple
Built by Monk Pu An in 1166 on Nanquan Mountain of Cihua Town, Yuanzhou District, it has received imperial inscriptions from emperors of the Song (960-1279), Yuan (1206-1368), Ming (1368-1644) and Qing (1644-1911) Dynasties.

杨岐普通寺

位于萍乡市杨岐山,初名广利禅寺,唐宝十二年(753年)由乘广禅师所创,宋庆历年间(1041~1048年),方会禅师在此创杨岐宗,将广利禅寺改名为普通寺。系中国佛教禅宗五宗七家之一临济宗杨岐派的发祥地。全寺依山而建,逐层递高,古朴雄伟。寺院由山门、弥勒佛殿、大雄宝殿、观音殿、祖师堂、客堂宿舍等建筑组成。

Putong Temple in Yangqi

Located in Yangqi Mountain of Pingxiang City, it was built by Monk Cheng Guang in 753 and named Guangli Temple. Monk Fang Hui established the Yangqi Sect of Buddhism here between 1041 and 1048 and changed the name to Putong Temple. It is the birthplace of Yangqi School of Linji Sect, one of the Five Sects and Seven Schools of Zen Buddhism in China.

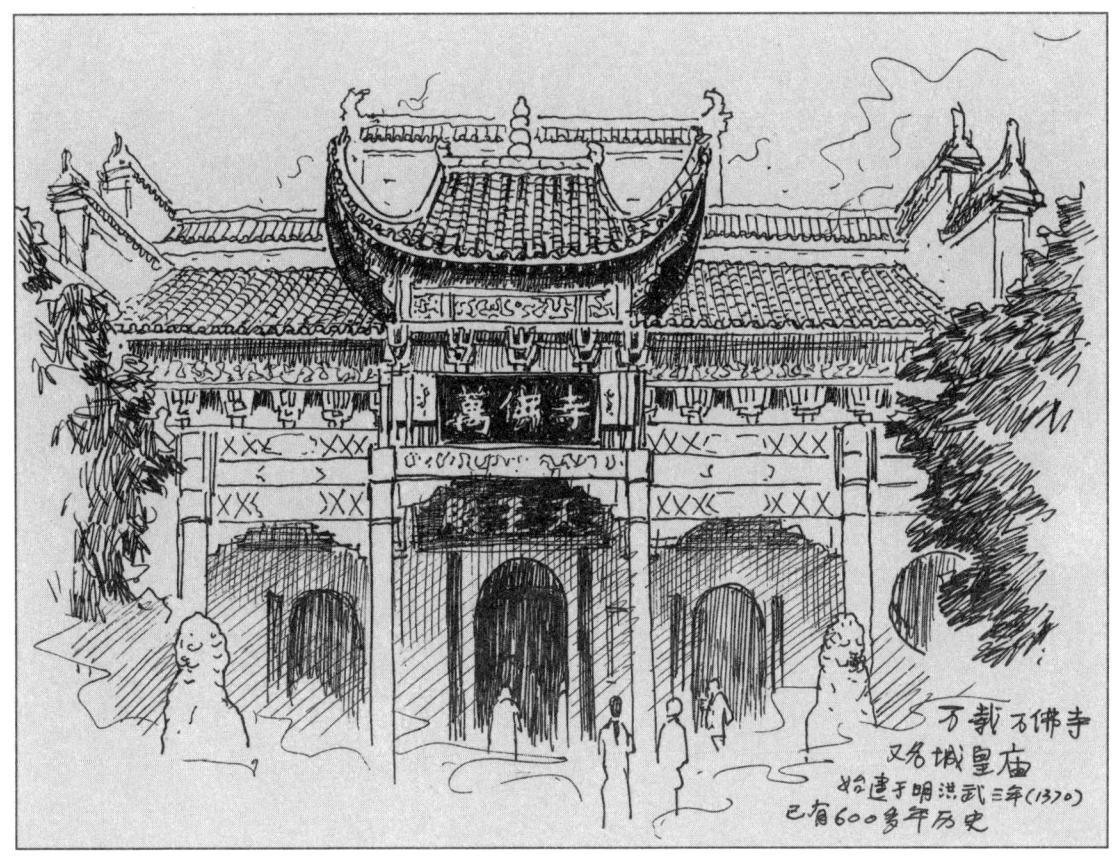

> 万载万佛寺
> 又名城隍庙
> 始建于明洪武三年(1370)
> 已有600多年历史

> 万佛庙

　　原为万载县城隍庙，位于万载县康乐街道龙河东岸集贤坊，始建于明洪武三年（1370年），由县丞冯厚礼以刘仁旧居改建。后历经多次战火损毁，历代均有重修。现存建筑为1997年重修，现名万佛寺，占地5000平方米。建筑古朴典雅，五进院落，气势壮观。

Wanfo Temple

Located in Jixian Lane, Kangle Street on the east bank of the Dragon River in Wanzai County, it used to be the Town God's Temple. First built in 1370 by the county chief Feng Houli at the site of Liu Ren's Mansion, it was damaged many times during years of warfare. Reconstructed in 1997, it was given its current name.

普利禅寺

位于宜丰县同安乡洞山村，始建于唐大中十三年（859年），由曹洞宗开山祖师良价所创，是禅宗五家之一曹洞宗的祖庭以及文化发祥地，这座千年古刹几经兴废，2010年复建。素有"洞天佛国，释家祖庭"的盛誉。

Puli Temple

Located in Dongshan Village of Tong'an Town in Yifeng County, it was founded in 859 by Monk Liang Jia, the founder of the Caodong Sect. It is the Zuting and birthplace of the Caodong Sect, one of the five sects of Zen Buddhism.

报恩寺旧址

　　位于袁州区东门泗州寺路与明月南路之间区域，据《袁州府志》载，宜春报恩寺从武周天授初年（690年）兴建"重兴寺"起，至少已有1320多年的历史，该寺毁于20世纪50年代。

Bao'en Temple

Located between Sizhousi and Southern Mingyue Roads near the East Gate of Yuanzhou, it was first built in 690 on the site of Chongxing Temple. After a history of over 1,320 years it was destroyed in the 1950's.

南禅塔

始建于宋元符巳卯年（1099年），附有南禅院，塔高七层，因修建浙赣铁路线而将塔拆毁于1936年。至今老火车站南侧还设有塔下村，此图为1998年根据90岁老人口述而忆画的。

Nanchan Pagoda

This seven-story pagoda and surrounding Nanchan Yard was founded in 1099 but razed in 1936 to build the Zhejiang-Jiangxi Railway. This sketch is based on the description a ninety year-old man.

文笔峰古塔

文笔峰是一座砖塔，因位袁州古城东，形状似竹笋，宜春人把它通俗化，称其为东门石笋，该塔始建于明天启二年（1622年），圆锥造型，高30米，内分七层，列级盘旋而上，原为宜春标志性景观，文笔峰的建成，大振宜春的文运，该塔毁于20世纪60年代。

Tower on Mount Wenbi

Located in the east corner of the old Yuanzhou, the cone-shape tower was first built in 1622. The seven floors of the 30-meters-tall tower were linked by spiral staircases. An iconic building of Yichun, it was destroyed in the 1960's.

万载文明塔

位于万载县城南门，始建于清乾隆十七年（1752年）。塔身由砖石砌成，通高约30米，共七层，下六层为六角形（底层为基座），最上一层为圆柱形，层与层相接处有腰檐挑出，七层之上是灰色圆锥形宝盖，盖上垒有塔刹。

Wenming Tower in Wanzai

Built in 1752 at the southern gate of Wanzai County, this seven-story brick-and-stone tower is 30 meters tall with a grey iconic canopy and spire.

雷火塔

位于宜春城北外环路北,塔高60多米,直径12米,共九层楼台,为八角形钢筋砼结构。它是美丽宜春和幸福宜春的标记,也是它自身内函与精神的标记。登高远望,春城美景尽收眼底。

Leihuo Tower

Located north of the Outer Ring Road of Yichun City, the seven-floor tower is over 60 meters tall and 12 meters in diameter. It is a symbol of the beautiful scenery and happy life in Yichun.

{ 昌山庙 }

位于分宜境内的袁河昌山峡西岸,坐西向东,于唐大和六年(832年)由宜春县令卢萼主持建造。千余年来几毁几修,信众远及方圆数百公里,特别是农历八月十三日龙母诞辰纪念日,香客云集,热闹非凡。

Changshan Temple
Facing east on the west bank of Changshan Gorge along the Yuanhe River in Fenyi, the temple was built in 832 under supervision of Lu E, county chief of Yichun. It was damaged several times over the past thousand years.

宜丰岳王庙

　　位于宜丰县城东郊，宋建炎四年（1130年）岳家军数度转战宜丰，期间运米赈济新昌饥民。为怀念岳家父子后人建庙祭祀。该庙始建于南宋，明清两代均有重修。

Yuewang Temple in Yifeng
Located in the eastern suburb of Yifeng County, the temple was built by his descendants in memory of Yue Fei, a patriotic general of the Southern Song Dynasty (1127-1279). In 1130, the Army of the Yue's Family passed Yifeng several times when on their way into battle. First built during the Southern Song Dynasty (1127-1279), it was rebuilt during the Ming (1368-1644) and Qing (1644-1911) Dynasties.

宜春文庙·大成殿（一）

位于丰城县丰城一中校园内，始建于南宋绍兴十三年（1143年），历代多次重修。原有建筑近一万平方米，有门、泮池、明伦堂、尊经阁、文昌宫、先代殿、启圣祠、乡贤祠、名宦祠、魁星阁、江山秀杰楼、斋署、龙山书院等建筑组成，历史上曾被誉为全国"三个半孔庙"之一，先仅存大成殿。

Confucius Temple in Yichun, Dacheng Hall (1)

Located on the grounds of the First High School of Fengcheng County, it was built in 1143 and renovated many times. Dacheng Hall is the only part pictured here.

宜春文庙·大成殿（二）

大成殿为重檐歇山顶建筑，上铺三色琉璃瓦，檐下密布计心造和偷心造斗拱，颇存宋代营造法式建筑遗意。大成殿高13.5米，进深16.6米，面阔22.5米，檐下有回廊，四周为红石质立柱26根。整个建筑气势宏大，结构精巧，是宜春古代最为著名的建筑之一。

Wenmiao Temple of Yichun · Dacheng Hall (2)

The hall is 13.5 meters high, 16.6 meters long and 22.5 meters wide. There are verandahs under the roofs and 26 red stone columns around the hall. Magnificent and exquisite, it is one of the most famous ancient buildings in Yichun.

宜春文昌宫

位于宜春市鼓楼路附近。当年袁州会议的参会人员均住在此。文昌宫何时建造不详,文昌宫主要是设立兴贤会,创置田租,资助乡会试路费及小试卷资,皆其首倡。

Wenchang Palace in Yichun

The palace was where participants of the Yuanzhou Conference stayed in September 29, 1930. The date of construction is unknown.

宜春化成寺

　　位于袁州区秀江河北岸化成岩森林公园内，始建于唐代唐朝宰相李德裕被贬袁州时，曾在该寺居住。寺院因战乱和自然灾害曾多次被毁。清咸丰六年（1856年）因兵废毁。后虽修复，却一直没有恢复元气，日渐式微。

Huacheng Temple in Yichun

Located in Huachengyan Forest Park on the north bank of Xiujiang River, in the western suburb of Yuanzhou District, it was first built during the Tang Dynasty (618-907) when Li Deyu, then Prime Minister, was banished to. Later, the temple was damaged by wars and natural disasters. In 1856 during the reign of Qing Emperor Xianfeng (1851-1862), it was largely destroyed in warfare. Despite later repairs, it has not regained its original elegance.

昌黎书院

位于袁州区宜春台右侧，为纪念唐代袁州刺史韩愈而建，于北宋皇祐五年(1053年)兴建韩文公祠以崇祀。元末被毁，后于嘉靖二十八年(1549年)以春台山东麓韩文公祠改建，改称"昌黎书院"。1914年，改为江西省立第八中学，现尚存一部分在宜春四中校园内。

Changli Academy

First built on the right side of Yichun Terrace in Yuanzhou District, it was in memory of Han Yu, the then governor of Yuanzhou during the Tang Dynasty (618-907). The Ancestor Hall of Han Yu was built here in 1053. It was destroyed at the end of the Yuan Dynasty (1206-1368) and rebuilt in 1549 based on Han Yu Ancestor Hall, which is on the east of Chuntai Mountain. Later its name was changed to Changli Academy.

状元洲读书堂（一）

　　亦名卢洲，位于宜春城区东侧，宜春大桥下游秀江中心。洲的东西长约800米，南北宽约200米，南北均距河岸100米，面积83亩。唐代文人卢肇在此苦读，后中状元，故曰状元洲。

Zhuangyuan Islet Study (1)

Also known as Luzhou, Zhuangyuan Islet is on the east side of Yichun District in the middle range of Xiujiang River below Yichun Bridge. Lu Zhao was a Tang (618-907) scholar studied here. He excelled in the imperial exam, taking the first place, thus the hall was named Zhuangyuan Islet.

状元洲读书堂（二）

明代邑人列聪在此建有"卢洲书屋"，清道光年间（1821~1850年）毁于洪水，1985年,状元洲被辟为水上公园,陆续筑有假山、水池、凉亭、牌楼等，修建了游泳池及娱乐游艺设施，并构建仿古建筑"卢肇读书堂"，辟"弋林斋"、"印月轩"，陈列部分书画作品及文物。复建书屋亭榭，使公园更具特色。

Zhuangyuan Islet Study (2)

Lie Cong of the Ming Dynasty (1368-1644) built Luzhou Study here. It was destroyed by flood but the area was expanded into a water park in 1985, with rockeries, ponds, summerhouses and decorated archways together with swimming pools and other amusement facilities. The classic building "Study of Lu Zhao" was established here.

> 苏家古祠

2003年宜春鼓楼路改造，改造前笔者用速写记下了待拆的苏家祠老屋。

Clan Hall of the Su's Family

This sketch made before Drum Tower Road of Yichun was reconstructed in 2003, is a sketch of the old structures of the Su Clan Hall.

> 竹坡公祠

　　位于分宜县宜介桥村,是明嘉靖年间(1522～1566年)首辅严嵩的故里,其祖祠名曰竹坡公祠,该祠主体建筑达600余年,曾几次修复都尽量保持历史原貌,介桥村已被列为江西省历史文化名村。

Zhupo Clan Hall

Located in Yijieqiao Village, Fenyi County, Xinyu City, it was the residence of Yan Song (1522-1566), a Prime Minister of the Ming Dynasty (1368-1644). Its main structure is more than 600 years old.

毓庆堂

　　介桥村严氏的"竹坡公祠"的堂名曰"毓庆堂",是介桥严氏第九世祖仲恭所建,祠堂主体为上下三进,堂内装饰雕琢精美,近百块古匾高雅夺目。其内装修极为考究,尤其是后殿内以隔断分成小室数间,其门或真或假,构思精妙,素有"小迷宫"之称。

Yuqing Hall

The Yan family's Zhupo Clan Hall in Qiaojie Village called Yuqing Hall was built by Zhong Gong, the ninth generation ancestor of the Yan Family in the village. Decorations inside are quite detailed, especially the rear hall divided into small chambers.

昌黎阁

位于宜春袁山顶端，是为纪念曾任袁州刺史的韩愈所建。建筑高21米，共三层，面积519平方米，一层为景韩堂；二层为恋清轩；三层为胜游楼。

Changli Building

Located atop Yuanshan Mountain in Yichun, it was built in memory of Han Yu, the governor of Yuanzhou. The three-story building is 21 meters high and with an area of 519 square meters.

老竹山的庐江堂

　　明月山旁的水口村花岩老竹山有一老祠屋名曰"庐江堂"，是何姓的祖祠，随一何氏嗣人前来拜祖访亲，故而写之。

Lujiang Hall on Laozhu Mountain

This is the He clan hall on Laozhu Mountain, Shuikou Village near Mingyue Mountain.

{ 朱氏节孝牌坊 }

位于宜春城南30千米的涧富村，为彰表夏思绶之妻朱氏而建造的，清代所建，四柱花岗石榫卯门楼石坊，檐下刻有"节孝"二字，并有"旌表大学士夏恩授之妻朱氏"12个字。夏思绶生于康熙年间，16岁考取功名并在京城为官，不幸18岁就去世了。其妻朱氏年仅14岁，未生育，后一直居住在夏家为夫守节，终生未再嫁。

Xia Memorial Arch

Located in Jianfu Village 30 kilometers south of Yichun City and built during the Qing Dynasty (1644-1911) in memory of Madam Xia, wife of Xia Sishou, this stone arch has four granite columns of mortise-tenon connections. Below the eave, are Chinese characters for integrity and piety engraved with twelve other characters meaning "Honor the spirit of Madam Xia".

袁京墓

宜春又名袁州，为纪念东汉高士袁京在此隐居并逝之故。山曰袁山，河曰袁河，郡曰袁州。袁京墓位于袁山西侧，其后裔重孙袁绍、袁术皆为三国名将。

Tomb of Yuan Jing

Yichun is also known as Yuanzhou, because of Yuan Jing, a talented scholar during the East Han Dynasty (25-220) who lived and died here. The mountains, rivers and city were all named after him. The tomb is west of Yuanshan Mountain. Yuan Shao and Yuan Shu, the great grandsons of Yuan Jing were both famous military leaders during the Three Kingdoms Period (220-280).

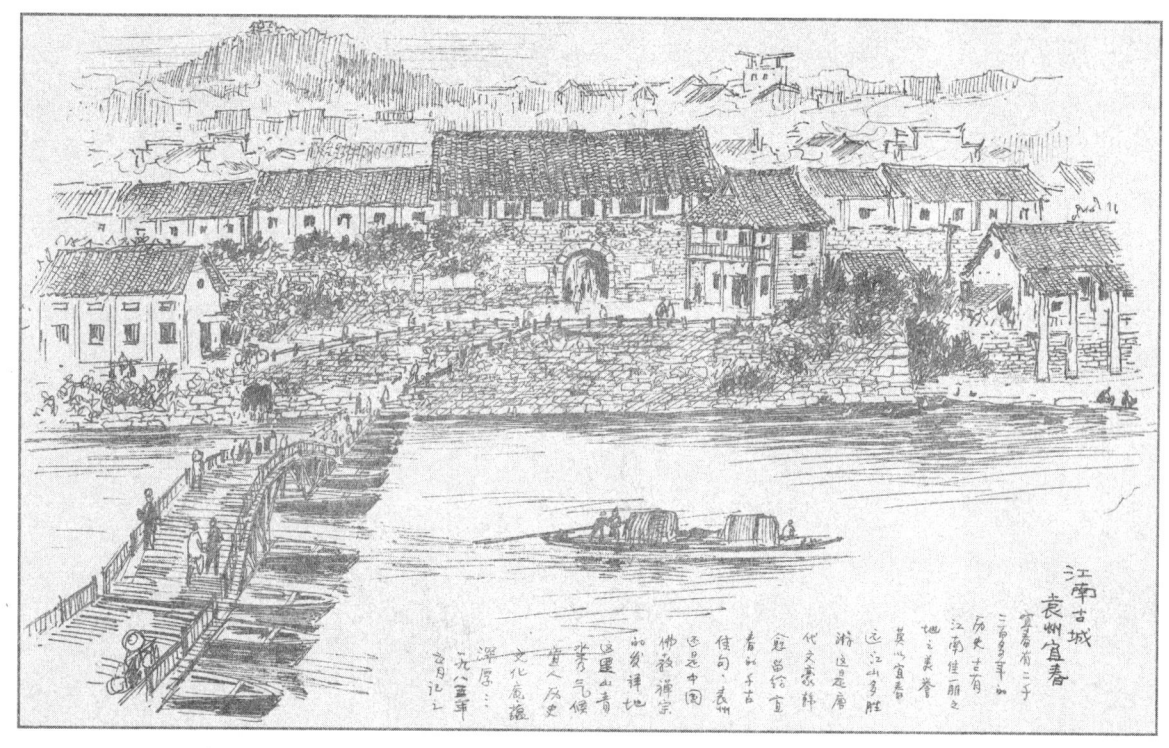

> 古城浮桥

　　古郡袁州宜春，自汉高祖六年（前201年）大将军灌婴定江南于此筑城建基，经过2200多年的沿革，可谓是亘古绵延，历史悠久。此地山青水秀，气候宜人，古有"江南佳丽之地"的美誉，此景为1983年古城"袁山门"前的浮桥情景。

Floating Bridge in the Ancient Town
Ancient Yichun has beautiful scenery and a pleasant climate. It is the site of the floating bridge in front of Yuanshan Mountain.

金鸡桥

位于铜鼓景区仙羊寨，建造虽不详，但桥头原立有一块明朝将领邓子龙题的"金鸡桥"石碑，桥头处还有一座金鸡桥古庙，钟磬上有"道光年间铸，武乡十九都"字样。

Jinji Bridge
Located in Xianyang Village in Tonggu Scenic Area, its construction date is unknown. At an end of the bridge, stood a stone tablet with an inscription by Deng Zilong, a Ming Dynasty (1368-1644) military leader.

<u>高安浮桥（一）</u>

  高安浮桥历史悠久，最早可追溯到五代十国时期杨吴乾贞二年（928年），取名永安桥，宋文豪苏辙有诗咏桥"虹腰宛转三百尺，鲸背参差十五舟"。笔者1979年来此，速写记录当时的浮桥南岸的情景。

Gao'an Floating Bridge (1)
Dating to 928, its original name was Yong'an Bridge. In 1979, the author made sketches of its southern end.

高安浮桥（二）

高安市区，一条锦河横穿南北两岸。河上有四座桥，其中一座是浮桥。1939年为适应对日作战将浮桥焚毁，1946年修复。1949年7月国民党军溃逃时将浮桥斩断缆绳放流。1951年县人民政府修复通行，全长161.85米，共14厢40只浮船组成。

Gao'an Floating Bridge (2)

Running from north to south through Gao'an District, the Jinghe River is crossed by four bridges, among which one was floating bridge. The 161.85-meter-long bridge consisting of 14 chambers and 40 floating boats was reopened after repair in 1951 by the county government.

上高浮桥

　　上高浮桥始建历史不详，1979年笔者来此速写记录了当时上高浮桥的一景。据有关资料记录，1981年上高浮桥因敖阳大桥落成而被拆除，实为一大憾事。今年又有许多群众呼吁重建浮桥。

Shanggao Floating Bridge
Its construction date unknown, the bridge was torn down in 1981 after completion of Aoyang Bridge. This sketch was made in 1979.

宜春砥柱桥

  位于宜春中村，桥的始建时期不清，桥头处有一碑刻，碑文中记载清光绪三十年（1904年）重修此桥之事，因字迹多处无法辩认。此桥四墩五孔，结构壮观。

Dizhu Bridge of Yichun

Located in Yichun Middle Village, its construction date unclear, it features a tablet inscription telling of its repair in 1904 during the reign of Qing Emperor Guangxu (1875-1909).

鸣水桥

位于宜春袁山公园。宜春大小袁山为古八景之一，大袁山西侧小湖中央的鸣水桥，洁白如玉，好一幅春色美景。

Mingshui Bridge

Located in Yichun Yuanshan park. Yuanshan is one of the ancient Eight Scenes of Yuanzhou.

升瀛桥

位于明月山下的刘坊村，昔日要登明月山，此桥为必经之路。据考证，此桥为清道光年间（1821~1850年）所建。

Shengying Bridge

The bridge was built between 1821 and 1850 on the only pass from Liufang Village to Mingyue Mountain.

大埠村石桥

　　位于袁州区温汤镇大埠村，该石桥约为清晚期所建。桥头处还有水车屋的残破旧房，古桥老屋都年久失修，面目不清了。

Stone Bridge in Dabu Village

Located in Dabu Village of Wentang Town in Yuanzhou District, it was built during the late Qing Dynasty (1644-1911). There are still some old waterwheel houses at the end of the bridge; Long without proper care, they are dilapidated.

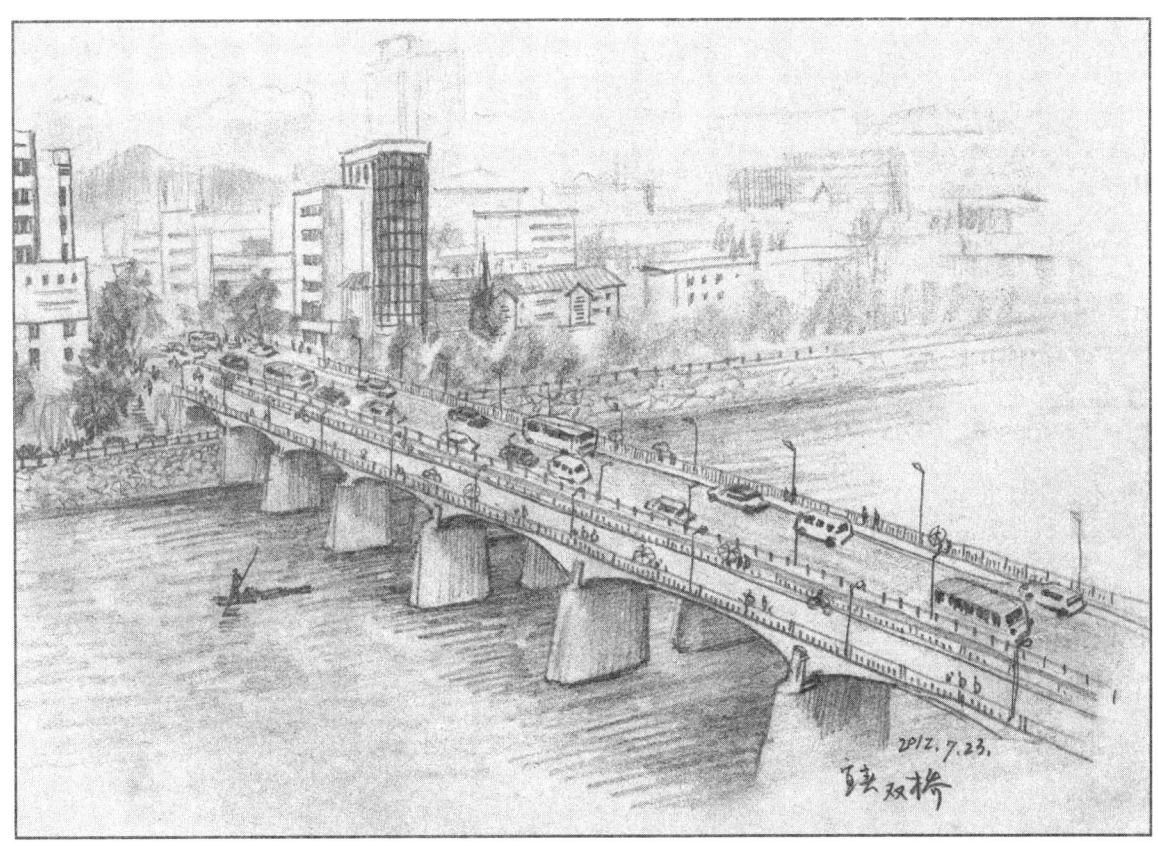

双 桥

位于在袁州区城西。据记载，1951年12月建成的秀江桥，长186米，因桥宽不足十米，满足不了交通需要，1984年10月在原秀江桥旁加建一桥合为双桥。

Double Bridge

Located west of Yuanzhou District, the first, Xiujiang Bridge, was finished in December 1951. It is 186 meters long and less than 10 meters wide. As it failed to meet the traffic demand, another bridge was added next to it in October 1984, thus the name Double Bridge.

永宁桥老街

铜鼓县的永宁桥为清雍正十二年（1734）所造，是三拱组成的两头台阶式的石拱桥，位于老街中段，这里是客家居民点。1979年我来此游览，写下了当时桥头老街一景。

Yongning Bridge Street
Built in 1734, the stone bridge consists of three arches with staircases at each end. It is in the middle session of Old Street, which is a major Hakka residence area. The author made this sketch during a visit in 1979.

潭山老街（一）

　　位于宜丰县潭山镇，潭山街之南有一座小山，早先伏溪水从山下经过，汇成一个深潭，山在潭岸上，故名潭山。宋朝以前，这里本是一片芦茅洲，并无村落，人们散居在东北茜槽一带山庄里。南宋时岳飞抗金转战此地，村落均被金兵破坏。后来一族刘姓兴村建市，发展很快。如今许多古街保存尚好，明清建筑风格甚浓。

Tanshan Street (1)

Located in Tanshan Town, Yifeng County, it used to be an island covered with wild reeds. There were no villages here until the Song Dynasty (960-1279), just folk scattered in mountains in Qiancao to the northeast. But a village developed quickly when the Liu clan began to help develop the market. Nowadays, many old streets are well preserved with distinctive Ming (1368-1644) and Qing Dynasty (1648-1911) features.

潭山老街（二）

潭山地处宜丰县北部，与修水、铜鼓、奉新三县交界，是历史上通往湘、鄂、赣的交通要道，千年古驿道必经之地。千百年来，特殊的地理区域，造就了潭山独有的建筑和民俗。

Tanshan Street (2)

At the border of Xiushui, Tonggu and Fengxin Counties, Tanshan is in north Yifeng County. Located on an ancient courier route, it was once a communication hub for Hunan, Hubei and Jiangxi Provinces. For a thousand years, distinctive customs and architectural styles developed here due to the unique geographic features.

潭山老屋

　　潭山老街的建筑均为土木结构，屋柱全是完整的树木制成，屋柱的基石雕化多样，美不胜收。但这些屋内人员稀少，据屋主人说，年轻人不愿住老屋，都去盖新大楼去了。

Houses in Tanshan

Buildings on Tanshan Street are of clay and wood, with columns of whole tree trunks. Cornerstones under these columns are decorated with varied exquisite patterns.

昌黎巷

位于袁州区,北起中山中路的东方街道办事处东侧巷口,南至韩家祠。1940年以唐代韩愈之籍贯叫昌黎巷。1968年更名东城巷。1982年复原名。袁州人民为了表达对韩愈的崇敬,把此巷称为昌黎巷。

Changli Lane

Located in Yuanzhou District, it runs from the Han Clan Hall in the south, to the east of Dongfang Neighborhood Office on Middle Zhongshan Road in the north. In 1940, local people named it Changli Lane in honor of Han Yu (768-824), a famous poet and Tang Dynasty official born in Changli.

> 下浦老街

位于袁州区老城东郊，昔日下浦为城郊，如今的下浦成了宜春城的中心区。图中的下浦小川老街，不久将从人们的视线中永远消失。

Xiapu Street

Located east of old Yuanzhou, Xiapu was once a suburb but now is the city center of Yichun. Below it is Xiaochun Street, which unfortunately will be demolished in the near future.

王子巷

位于袁州区，南起中山中路，北至小北门。清乾隆四十九年（1784年）后为宜春南北交通要道（因老秀江桥倒塌，新秀江桥正对小北门即王子巷）。西汉元光六年（前129年），汉武帝封长沙定王刘发之子刘成为宜春侯，后人建王子庙于此，世称王子巷。1966年改新风巷。1982年5月复原名。

Prince Lane

In Yuanzhou District, ranging from Middle Zhongshan Road in the south to Xiaobei Gate in the north, it has been the major north-south route in Yichun since 1784. In 129 BC, Han Emperor Hanwu awarded Liu Cheng (son of Liu Fa, a high-ranking official of Changsha) the title Prince of Yichun. The prince's temple was built here; the lane is named after it.

泉井头老巷

宜春的泉井头巷还保留一大片低矮老屋,虽然又挤又密但相互错落有致,在此生活惯了的老居民还舍不得搬走。

Quanjingtou Lane

Many low and old houses remain in Quanjingtou Lane. They are crowded but in a good arrangement. Many residents are reluctant to move out.

潮溪村

位于温汤镇的潮溪村,村口有一老村门,有着600余年的历史。去年来此采访,听当地村民讲了不少该村文人武士的故事。村头的一条小溪穿村而过,水质清彻透明。

Chaoxi Village

Located in Wentang Town, the village gate has a history of over 600 years. I heard a lot of the story about scholars and military figures in the village during my interview with the local people.

新昌镇

　　位于宜丰县，初名盐步镇，建立于南唐保大十年（952年），因此地有盐溪、盐岭、盐洞、盐洲、盐台五盐之名，又为河运之步（埠）头，故名。自宋代建新昌县以来，新昌一向为县治所在，地域分属泰和乡和义钧乡。1914年因与浙江新昌县同名改为宜丰县。

Xinchang Town

Located in Yifeng County, it was originally known as Yanbu Town when built in 952. It has been the county seat since the establishment of Xinchang County during the Song Dynasty (1368-1644). In 1914, it was renamed Yifeng to avoid name duplication with another county in Zhejiang Province.

> 易家老屋

位于万载县严坑村，建造年代不详，据村里人讲已有百年历史、这记载着家族兴衰的百年老屋向人们静静的诉说着历史的沧桑，正可谓"墙体裂痕记岁月，门联刻字见性情。百年老屋楼空静，明清风格韵尚存"。

Yi Clan Houses

Located in Yankeng Village, Wanzai County, their construction date is unknown, but according to local residents, they date back more than 100 years.

锦江河边老屋

  位于万载县城锦江河边，故地不成样，建造年代不详，远远看去也有百年以上历史。这里码头人稀少，弧河自流长。村外高楼起，矮屋要扫光。在此留个影，速写记一方。此图为1989年的老屋群情景。

Houses at Jingjiang River

Located at Jinjiang River, Wanzai County, the construction date of these dilapidated buildings is unknown. The dock area along the along this river bend is sparsely populated. This sketch is a 1989 view.

袁州老屋

　　位于袁州区宜春二小校门口，为民国时期所建的老屋，三层建筑。当时袁州三层高的楼房并不多，一楼为临街店铺，楼房的窗花、木雕、走廊很是讲究，很有特色。

House in Yuanzhou

Not far from the Yichun Second Primary School in Yuanzhou District, it was built during the Republic of China Period (1912-1949). The first of its three floors is a shop with distinctive stylish lattice windows woodcarvings and verandahs.

高安石脑老屋

前年四月我来高安石脑丁家拜访一位远亲。主人指着自己的老祠堂说:"祠堂成了危房,自己无钱修理,总有一天会倒掉。"我看此屋很有特色,敬而速写记之。

House in Shinao of Gaoan

When I visited a distant relative in Shinao, the owner of a clan hall told me, "It is rated as dilapidated, but I don't have the money to revamp it. Sooner or later it will collapse." I felt pity for this distinctive house; so, I immediately sketched it.

> 废弃的水车屋

宜春河道颇多,旧时自然多水车,历经世事变迁大都废弃不用,留下破败的水车,每每看到总有万千感慨:"昔日水车屋,如今几残木,溪水弧自流,漏液似泪哭。"

Waterwheel Houses

Many waterwheel houses were built in Yichun, which is crossed by rivers. The majority of them are abandoned. Every time I see them, I am touched.

化成岩下的农舍（一）

位于袁州区市区西郊、秀江北岸。化成岩下的农户大多为菜农，2000年期间这里还可见到成片的菜地，如今图中的所描的景象均被高楼大厦所代替。

Cottages under Huacheng Cliff (1)

Located in the western suburb of Yuanzhou District on the north bank of Xiujiang River, they are home to farmers, most of whom grow and sell vegetables. Large areas of vegetable fields seen before 2000 have been replaced by tall buildings, as shown in this sketch.

化成岩下的农舍（二）

这里被誉为"江南一胜"和"天然图画"。每当渔舟唱晚，牧笛催归之际，古寺钟声，悠扬清越，回荡在寥廓江天，城郊内外，清晰可闻，给人清静幽远之感。在这里居住的人们真正是"采菊东篱下，悠悠见南山"。

Cottages under Huacheng Cliff (2)

This site is known as one of the beautiful scenes in South China. In tranquility, residents here embrace nature and enjoy beautiful scenery and an easy life.

滩下路的老屋

路位于宜春城东,秀江河的上游,昔时这里的居民以河边的沙滩围作田,故名滩下路,如今城区秀江两岸高楼密布,田和菜地都消失殆尽。

Houses on Tanxia Road

Located east of Yichun on the upper reaches of Xiujiang River, they were home to farmers who turned riversides into farmland. The Road is named after that activity (Tanxia means along the river bank.). But nowadays, tall buildings crowd the riverbank and the rice paddies and vegetable plots are gone.

凤凰山下居民区

宜春的凤凰山下原是工程机械厂厂区,该厂迁走后设为七家岭社区,不少房地产开发商盯上了这块宝地。这张速写记录了居民生活区的一角。

Community at the foot of Phoenix Mountain

Once a machinery plant site, the area was converted into Qijialing Community when the plant was removed. Real estate developers were keen to develop it. This sketch is a corner of residence there.

东城巷居民区

位于袁州区的考棚路连接东城巷路，居民称东山角里。此处有多栋20世纪50、60年代的老楼房，在此住了几十年的居民正盼望房屋改造。满足住上新楼房的心愿。

Dongchengxiang Community

Located on Kaopeng Road, Yuzhou District, it borders Dongchengxiang Road. It is known as Dongshanjiao Lane by locals living here in many houses built in the 1950's and 1960's. They long for renovation or relocation.

三眼古井

宜春的古井形式多样，有三眼井、四眼井、五眼井、七眼井等等，其实这些多眼井的底部都是一口大井，多眼井只是可供多人同时取水，井然有序，方便又卫生，三眼井的原址在步步高大厦处，毁于1990年。

Sanyan Well

Yichun is famous for its different kinds of wells, including those with three, four, five, and even seven outlets. Actually, they are linked to a single aquifer underground. They are a convenient source for clean water.

七眼古井

位于袁州区朝阳路七眼井巷13号,至今尚保留完好,井水仍然清亮透明,冬暖夏凉,清凉爽口,不过如今自来水普及,直接饮用井水者很少。井旁洗衣、洗菜者还非常热闹。

Seven-Outlet Well

Located at No. 13 Qiyanjing Lane, Chaoyang Road, Yuanzhou District, it is very well preserved. Warm in winter and cool in summer, the water is as clear as ever but tap water is widely used today, few locals drink the well water.

宜春耶稣堂

位于宜春市袁州区红星路的坡顶上,始建于清光绪三十年(1904年),由英籍传教士骆济世牧师奉命派遣来宜春购地所建,总建筑面积3000平方米。

Chapel in Yichun

Located a top of a hill on Hongxing Road, Yuanzhou District, Yichun, it was built in 1904 by Jishi Luo a British missionary sent to Yichun to buy land for its construction.

安源煤矿·总平巷

位于萍乡市,建于清光绪二十四年(1898年),为清末邮传大臣、官商盛宣怀为解决汉阳铁厂燃料之需,引进外资和西方先进采矿技术开发的。为中国近代经济建设立下了汗马功劳。它是中国工人运动的策源地、秋收起义的主要爆发地,也是中国近代煤炭工业化程度最高的煤炭基地之一,具有悠久的历史文化内涵。总平巷为该矿井的主要出入口。

Anyuan Coal Mine - Zongping Lane
Built in Pingxiang City in 1898, it is one of the birthplaces of the Chinese Workers' Movement, and the Autumn Harvest Uprising. One of the most industrialized coal production bases in modern China, it has rich historical and cultural significance. Zongping Lane is the major entrance.

袁州会议旧址

位于袁州区东风大街22号，原系张天成国药店，后栋正厅为会议旧址。1930年9月29日，在此召开了红一方面军总前委会议，史称"袁州会议"。毛泽东、朱德、朱云卿、杨岳彬、黄公略、蔡会文、林彪、罗荣桓、彭德怀、滕代远、邓萍、张纯清、吴灌之、袁国平、李井泉等参加了会议，同日发布了向吉安进军的命令。

Site of the Yuanzhou Conference
Located at No. 22 of Dongfeng Street, Yuanzhou District, it was once the pharmacy of Zhang Tiancheng. In September 29, 1930, in the main hall of the rear building, the Yuanzhou Military Conference of the First Red Army was held here.

铜鼓人民英雄碑

1979年8月出差铜鼓，午饭后利用休息时间完成了此幅速写。

Monument to the People's Heroes in Tonggu

The author made this sketch during a lunch break in August 1979 when he was on a business trip to Tonggu.

玻璃厂的老烟囱

　　昔日风光一时的宜春威昌玻璃厂已成为破旧的空厂房和几堆锈迹斑斑的废铁，无语的烟囱显得孤苦零丁。

Weichang Glass Factory Chimneys
Only dilapidated, empty workshops, iron scrap and silent chimneys remain.

自然风光
Natural Landscape

铜鼓石

位于铜鼓县城东1000米帅家坝境内,又名试剑石,石高十余米,形如铜鼓,石峭壁上刻有"铜鼓石"三字落款为备兵使者延论书,为铜鼓营城八景之一,铜鼓县也因此石而得名。另外还有试剑、潘周过化等字,为明朝将领邓子龙所题。

Tonggu Stone

Located in Shuaijiaba, 1,000 meters east of Tonggu County, it is also known as the Sword Testing Stone. 10 meters high in the shape of a drum, it was engraved by Yan Lun, a military envoy, with three Chinese characters: Tong Gu Shi meaning Copper Drum Stone. It is among the eight most magnificent historic sites in Tonggu.

上高锦江河边

锦江河为上高县的母亲河，秀水东流，风光旖旎，木舟穿流、渔歌阵阵，速写记实，记忆犹新。

Jinjiang Riverbanks, Shanggao County

The mother river of Shanggao County, the Jinjiang River has beautiful scenery, singing fishermen and floating wood boats. It deeply impressed me.

仰山·千年古杏

　　仰山坐落于武功山脉的一条支脉上，距离宜春城约40千米，因其山势"高耸万仞，可仰不可登"而得名。仰山的南惹有一山门江湖古道，山门左右有两棵参天银杏大树。据了解，两银杏一公一母，牵手千年，树龄达1800余年，真是活的化石。

Yanshan Mountain• Apricots

In Nanre, Yanshan Mountain, an ancient path leading to a temple gate is sheltered by two towering apricot trees on each side. It is said that one is male and one female. Facing each other for 1,800 years, they are considered living fossils.

仰山·梯田

　　唐宋时期，宜春地区出现了垦荒热潮，"大田耕尽却耕山"。据史书记载，袁州仰山岭坡上都是稻田，称为梯田。史书中最早出现"梯田"的名词且是宜春仰山。

Yanshan Mountain terrace fields

During the Tang (618-907) and Song (960-1279) Dynasties, there was much land reclamation in Yichun. According to historical records, all paddy fields on Yangshan Mountain were terraces. It is said terrace fields first appeared in Yangshan, Yichun.

明月山·小景

明月山主要由太平山、玉京山、老山、仰山等十几座海拔千米以上的山峰组成，因整个山势呈半圆形，恰似半轮明月，故称明月山。其景色优美，处处皆景。有感于此，附小诗一首"亲水游山得心静，写图描景赏眼新，行脚多广勤于笔，观物醉情墨乃清。"以赞其丽。

Mingyue Mountain Scenic Location

It includes Taiping, Yujing, Lao and Yangshan Mountains, all of which are thousands of meters high. Their half moon arrangement gives birth to the name.

明月山·竹林月影

　　明月山位于宜春市西南15千米处，是佛教发源地之一，禅宗的五大宗派之一沩仰宗就发源于此。"竹林月影"是明月山进山路口的休闲场所，集茶艺、书画、民乐、餐饮于一体，徽派建筑，装饰优雅，融山水为一体，清静诱人。

Mingyue Mountain - Bamboo Shadow in Moonlight

15 kilometers southwest of Yichun City, Mingyue Mountain is one of the birthplaces of Chinese Buddhism, and the cradle of the Weiyang Sect (one of the five Sects of Buddhism). Bamboo Shadow in Moonlight is the name of a leisure facility at the mountain base.

明月山·云谷飞瀑

是明月山五叠瀑布的第一瀑布"云谷飞瀑",为宜春古八景之一,此瀑布长达160米,乃为江西第一高瀑,蔚为壮观。清朝诗人江为龙有诗云:"轻烟漠漠锁山腰,一道泉流玉屑飘,气吐白虹晴欲雨,瀑飞翠壁夜闻潮……"

Mingyue Mountain - Yungu Falls

The most famous of the Five Falls of Mingyue Mountain, it is among the Eight Historic Sites of Yichun. At 160 meters, it is the highest in Jiangxi Province.

> 洪江山林小景

　　洪江乡地处丰城市海拔最高的山区，全境山峦起伏，境内最高点为西部的鸡龙山主峰。境内山色秀美，乡景迷人，我与几位族人来此探亲访友，酒店窗外小景使我忍不住拿起了画笔。

Hongjiang Forest Site in Hongjiang Town
Mountain scenery in Hongjiang is beautiful. It deeply impressed me when I visited there. I attracted by the beautiful scene outside our hotel; thus, I made this sketch.

84

状元洲旧景

昔日状元洲没有什么大建筑，除状元读书堂之外，内有一个小花圃、游泳池、跑马场等。这是写于1999年状元洲的速写。

Zhuangyuan Islet Site

There used to be few big buildings here, except for Zhuangyuan Study composed of garden, swimming pool and racecourse. The sketch was made in 1999.

筒车悠悠

千年筒车乐悠悠，灌溉农田不停留，欢歌唱得丰收景，世代为民写春秋。这是2003年5月写于宜春下浦龙家筒车的情景。

Waterwheels

For thousands of years, waterwheels in Yichun pumping irrigation water continuously. People celebrated the autumn harvest with song and word. This sketch is of waterwheels in the Long Clan's Xipu Village in Yichu.

袁河岸边小景

袁河流入城区，人们称之为秀江河，两岸绿带成荫，亭阁多样。成双成对的结伴人群，游岸散心，谈情说爱，散步观光，悠哉自由。

Sight at Yuanhe River

This tree and pavilion-decorated section of the Yuanhe River is known as Xiujiang River.

市郊边山路小景

20世纪末,这里是原油茶林场的杂乱旧房,如今这些景象无影无踪了。有一位老工人看到我的速写,连忙拿去复印留作纪念。

Suburban Mountain Path Site

At the end of the 20th Century, this site included ramshackle structures of a camellia farm, but they have now been completely destroyed. A worker who saw my sketch of it asked me for a souvenir copy of it.

民风民俗
Folk Customs

三角班

三角班，在江西抚州、吉安等地又称之为采茶戏。是赣中、赣西一带一种主要由"生、旦、丑"三个角色组成的富有乡土气息的汉族民间小戏，距今已有近两百年的历史。

Sanjiaoban Opera

Sanjiaoban is known as Tea-Picking Opera in Fuzhou and Ji'an cities of Jiangxi Province. It is a 200-year-old ethnic Han rural opera, with male, female and clown roles.

三星鼓乐

　　宜春三星鼓是一种汉族民间器乐演奏形式,又名三声鼓,是一种地地道道的汉族传统民乐。由农民演奏,供农村婚丧喜事使用。宜春三星鼓起源于明朝,有200余年的历史,是宫廷鼓乐派生出来的一种器乐演奏形式,民族气息浓郁,取民间福、禄、寿三星高照之意而得名。

Sanxing Drum Music

Sanxing Drum Music in Yichun is an ethnic Han performance of musical instruments also known as Sansheng Drum performance. Peasants play this at weddings and funerals. It originated during the Ming Dynasty (1368-1644) with a history of over 300 years.

> 万载傩舞

　　始于元末明初，盛行于明代初年，以客家地区的潭埠镇为最，在潭埠镇的沙江桥，还保存着专门供奉傩神的傩庙，傩庙分上下两个厅，上厅较小，供奉傩神，下厅较大，为演练傩舞的地方。正月跳傩的风俗在万载源远流长，万载傩舞被誉为"中国古代舞蹈活化石"。

Wanzai Nuo Dance

Dating back to the late Yuan (1206-1368) and the early Ming (1368-1644) Dynasties, it enjoyed its heyday in the early years of the Ming Dynasty (1368-1644). Tanbu Town inhabited by the Hakkas was especially famous for the dance. Performing Nuo dance in January of Chinese lunar calendar is a longtime tradition, while Nuo Dance in Wanzi is considered a Living Fossil of China's ancient dances.

春锣艺人

　　身披红带,一边打着小锣一边唱着小曲调。每到一户门前则递上一张春耕节气图,卖艺换钱,这是旧时的春锣艺人。据记载,这是乾隆皇帝下江南体察民情时演变出来的一种乡俗。

Artists Performing Spring Gong
Bedecked with red ribbons, artists sang and played the gong (Chunluo in Chinese) and distributed maps of the solar terms for Spring farming advice. They made money in this way with their skills. This is a picture of Chunluo artists in the olden days.

舞龙队

舞龙俗称玩龙灯，是一种中国的汉族传统民俗文化活动之一。舞龙时，龙跟着绣球做各种动，穿插，不断地展示扭、挥、仰、跪、跳、摇等多种姿势。宜春的节庆喜事都有舞龙的习俗。

Dragon-Dance Team

Called Playing Dragon Lantern, it is a traditional Chinese cultural activity. Yichun folk enjoy it during festival and family celebrations.

脱胎漆器

宜春脱胎漆器为中国四大"脱胎漆器"之一,创始于东汉时期,距今至少也有1700多年历史。其造 型美观,轻巧玲珑,色泽明丽,光亮如镜。清末南洋赛会上喜获银奖。誉名国内外,为"袁州三宝之一",是江西省著名手工艺产品之一。

Baseless Lacquer ware

The baseless lacquer ware of Yichun is one of the four major baseless lacquer wares in China. With a 1,700-year, it is one of the three treasures of Yuanzhou and a famous handicraft of Jiangxi Province.

手工夏布

宜春夏布始于唐宋时期,有上千年的历史,一向以"柔软润滑,平如水镜,轻如罗绡"响誉国内外,尤其受日本、韩国用户所喜爱,为"袁州三宝之一"。

Handmade Xia Cloth

First made during the Tang (618-907) and Song (960-1279) Dynasties, it has a history of thousands of years. Popular in China and aboard, it is particularly loved by Japanese and South Koreans. It is one of the Three Treasures of Yuanzhou.

松花皮蛋厂

宜春的松花皮蛋从清光绪年间起就开始生产,已有100余年的历史。其蛋白晶莹透明,松花图案美妙,味美芳香,清净可口,独具一格,深受国内外顾客欢迎,为"袁州三宝之一"。

Preserved-Egg Workshop

Preserved egg production began during the reign of Qing Emperor Guangxu (1875-1909). Its products are popular in China and aboard and are rated as one of the Three Treasures of Yuanzhou.

乡村谷酒

宜春的酒曾作为上等贡品进贡皇帝,《新唐书·地理志》载"(宜春)有宜春泉,酿酒入贡"。北宋大文学家苏东坡曾写下"闻道美酒出宜春,才倾一盏已醺人"的佳句。

Village-Made Rice Wine
Yichun rice wine was once chosen as tribute to the imperial court. Su Dongpo, a great man of letters during the Northern Song Dynasty (960-1127) wrote poems praising it.

车葫芦工艺

　　手工木制车葫芦见得不多了。这种工艺大多被机械化所代替。工艺容易失传的主要原因是年轻人不肯学。

Che Gourd Handicraft

Handmade Che Gourds are not often seen nowadays. Most are now machine-made and the tradition is almost lost because younger generations are reluctant to learn it.

> 弹棉工艺

    弹棉工艺自元朝就有，工具有大木弓，用牛筋为弦，还有木槌、铲头、磨盘等。弹时，用木槌频频击弦，使板上棉花渐趋松散。如今手工弹棉逐步添加机械设施，很少听到那种嗡吧作响富有节奏的弹棉声了。。

Cotton Fluffing Technique

This technique developed during the Yuan Dynasty (1206-1368). Due to the increasing use of mechanical devices, the rhythmic sound of traditional cotton fluffing is less often heard.

水豆腐（一）

　　宜春泉水好，当然豆腐也就味美佳，尤其是水豆腐更受老百姓喜爱，大街小巷均有水豆腐的叫卖声，此食品清热爽口，老少皆宜。

Soft Bean Curd (1)

The good quality of water in Yichun has contributes to the distinct taste of the bean curd popular among the locals and vendors can be seen everywhere. Cool and tasty, it is popular among all age groups.

水豆腐（二）

这滑嫩可口、不可多得的美食在旧时卖水豆腐的商贩遍布宜春的大街小巷，现今只能偶尔看到挑着木桶叫卖水豆腐的身影。

Soft Bean Curd (2)

Bean curd vendors, common in Yichun in the old days, are now only occasionally seen peddling bean curd from their barrels on the street.

> 烟花鞭炮

　　株潭镇是万载县传统花爆产业大镇，占全县花爆业的近三分之一，而且产品多样，深受用户喜爱。

Fireworks and Firecrackers

Zhutan Town, Wanzai County, a major producer of fireworks and firecrackers, produces about one third of the county's output. A great variety of its products are very popular among customers.

清明祭祖

每年的清明节我都会回老家参加集体扫墓活动。每到此时，老屋祠堂内都摆满了餐具等物品，同族人一起扫完墓后集体用餐，这是用餐前的厅堂情景。

Worship Ritual for Ancestral Tomb-Sweeping Day

For the annual Tomb-Sweeping Day, I go back to my hometown to sweep the tombs. Tableware and other items are put in the clan halls. After the sweeping ritual in which every family member participates, the family dines together. This is a sketch of the dining room before the meal.

庙会集市

是一种传统的物资交流方式，这种贸易方式延续至今。每逢大的节假日，宜春各地都会举行各种形式的庙会集市。

Temple Fair

This is a traditional process of goods exchange that continues today. Many temple fairs are held in Yichun during holidays.

街头陶瓷品

景德镇的陶瓷工艺品走出厂家，远道而来在宜春公园等地举行展销活动。陶瓷的特点是不怕水，露天展销不怕雨。在此经过，欣然止步而写之。

Ceramic Works in Street

The ceramics manufacturers hold trade fairs in Yichun Park and elsewhere in Jingdezhen. I sketched this scene while visiting a street fair.

杂品市场

　　生活用品千万种，能想得到的东西也许就能做得出来，小生意可生大财富。因此，采购销售要与民生紧密相关，经商的大学问就在此。

Sundry Goods Market
Daily goods are supplied in a large numbers. You name it; the market has it. Small businesses do a good profit selling them.

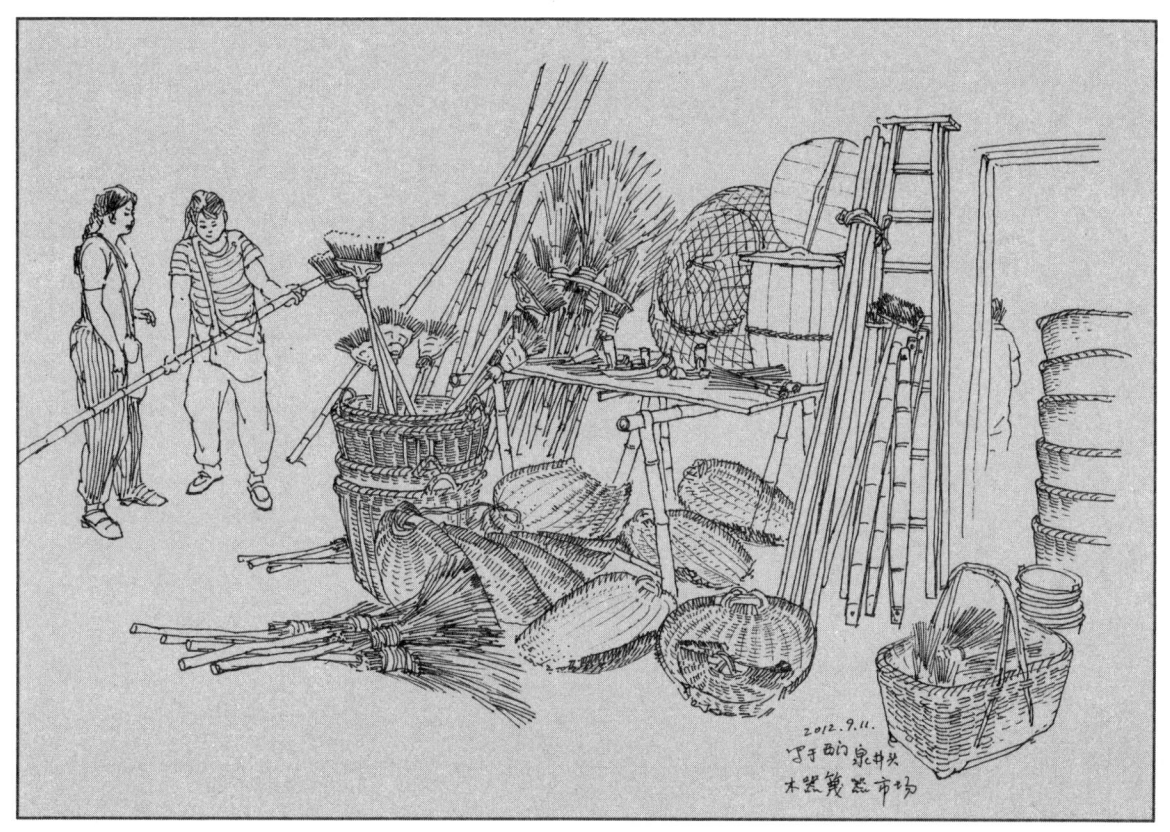

竹木杂品

宜春是毛竹之乡,竹木资源丰富,竹篾器、木器产品也丰富多样。宜春西门的泉井头设有竹木篾器专供市场,这是市场买卖现场速写。

Sundry Products of Bamboo and Wood

Yichun is rich in mao bamboo, and famous for the variety of bamboo utensils and other wooden products. A market, specifically of bamboo and wood utensils, was set up in Quanjingtou, near Yichun's western gate. This is a sketch of the market there.

> 杂货店

虽然是杂货品多，但分门别类排列有序，自然形成一种疏密有度的节奏韵律。加上房主是一位九十多岁和气生财之人，我坐下来越画越有滋味。

Groceries
Grocery stores here are clearly categorized and well arranged. I enjoyed making friends with this nice storeowner in his nineties as I sketched him.

宜春汉春祥骑楼杂货店

　　会做生意就可能会做人，会做人就能立一个家，能立家者当然就是成功之人，这个老字号杂货店几十年不衰，当然与主人经营有方，经商理念分不开。

Arcade Grocery in Hanchunxiang, Yichun

A good businessman is a decent fellow who can keep his family in a good order and, therefore, sure to be successful. The long-lasting prosperity of this time-honored grocery cannot be achieved without the good management practices and business philosophy of its owner.

称 店

从秦始皇时代开始统一度量衡,秤的历史延续至今。古秤的工艺还在使用,电子秤的应用逐渐普及,制秤师傅要跟时代,也要与时俱进不断学习。

Weight Measurement Scales (Steelyards) Store

Steelyards have been used in China since Emperor Qin (259-210BC) unified the measurement systems. Though steelyards are still used, electronic scales are more popular today.

> 春台菜市场

  春台公园位于宜春城的中心,据称公园门口的菜市场自古设台以来就有,应该有一两千年的历史。这里一天到晚人群川流不息,叫卖声不断。来此登台的人往往都喜欢到市场里去走走,体察一下这里的风俗人情。

Vegetable Market in Chuntai Park

Located at the center of Yichun, the market at the gate of the park is said to have existed since the establishment of Yichun Terrace; so it has a history of 100 to 200 years.

殷家蔬果市场

宜春城南的殷家，大多为菜农居民，在家门口摆上菜摊，一是新鲜，二是品种齐全，三是价格合理。吸引了不少远道而来的采购者。此菜摊的排列组合本身就是一件艺术作品，且迫使我停下脚步画个仔细。

Yin Clan Vegetable and Fruit Market

A majority of the Yin Clan living in southern Yichun are vegetable farmers, who lay out products for sale near their homes attracting customers from afar, with freshness, variety and reasonable prices.

箭道市场

　　箭道市场就是春台公园门口市场的总称，这个画面是西侧路的情景，九、十月是黄豆盛产的季节。

Jiandao Market

This is the general name for all markets at Chuntai Park Gate. This is a sketch of the street on the western side. September and October is the season to harvest soybeans.

乐在其中

　　擦皮鞋、修车辆，人力车等也有结帮行为，有时候他们同吃同干，做累了又在一起玩耍，乐在其中，场面生动。

Enjoying Life

Shoe polishers, auto mechanics and rickshaw drivers collaborate and work, eat and enjoy leisure time together after a busy day.

大坪巷的早点摊

　　大坪巷居民密集,直通中山路大街,路口上的早点摊位生意繁忙。夫妻协作井条有序,口感好,品种多,又卫生,服务又热情,大家都成为这里的常客。

Breakfast Stalls in Daping Lane
Daping Lane is a densely populated district adjoining Zhongshanlu Street. Breakfast stalls in the lane are popular among the locals.

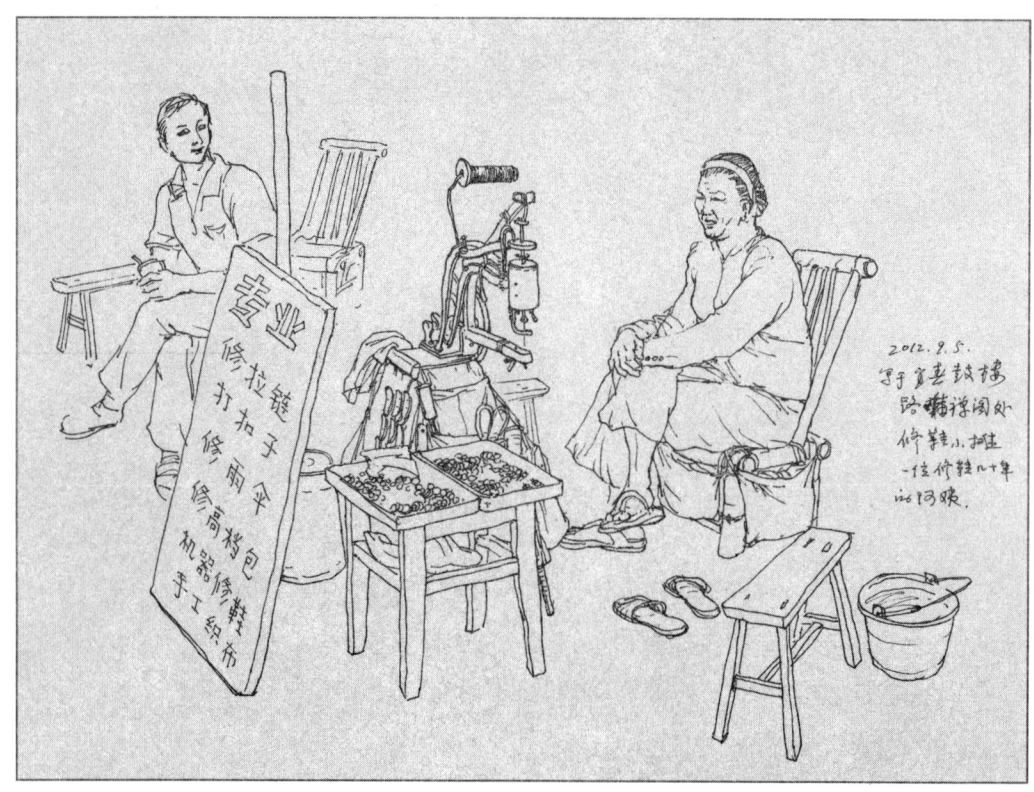

缝补小摊位

缝补修鞋几十年，知艰识苦养一家。从阿姨脸上的皱纹中可以读出她生活的艰辛，从她可亲的笑容中又知其精神世界是非常乐观的。

Stalls for Sewing and Mending
Sewing and mending for decades, the women know much about the hardships of supporting a family. The facial wrinkles tell her story; the amiable smile shows her optimism.

> 温汤泡脚广场

　　温汤镇是长寿之乡，人们发现这与温泉有直接的关系。因此，从解放初期开始，这里就建有各种温泉疗养所。如今的古井泡脚广场，已成为温汤的一道风景线。

Foot-Spa Square, Wentang Town

Wentang is known for the longevity of its people which is said to be linked to the hot springs here. Foot-Spa Square is a scenic area of the town nowadays.

温汤古井

温汤古井长三米，宽二米，仅六平方米，竟可满足上万人同时泡脚，这也是个奇迹。富晒矿泉，水温平均68～72摄氏度，能饮能浴，能满足人们生活中的各方需求。因此，有不少大都市的人还在温汤置房长住，养生休闲，以泉乡为家了。

Wentang Town Well

The well is three meters long and two meters wide - an area of only six square meters; it can accommodate many people for a foot SPA at the same time. The average water temperature varies from 68 to 72 degrees Celsius.

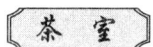

茶室

茶好静心，物美养人。茶室的环境设施可以调理一个人的性情，中国传统的竹木家俬最具人性化。

Tea Room

Tea cultivates tranquility of mind and the beautiful environment in a tearoom helps improve one's character. The traditional bamboo furniture of China is enjoyable.

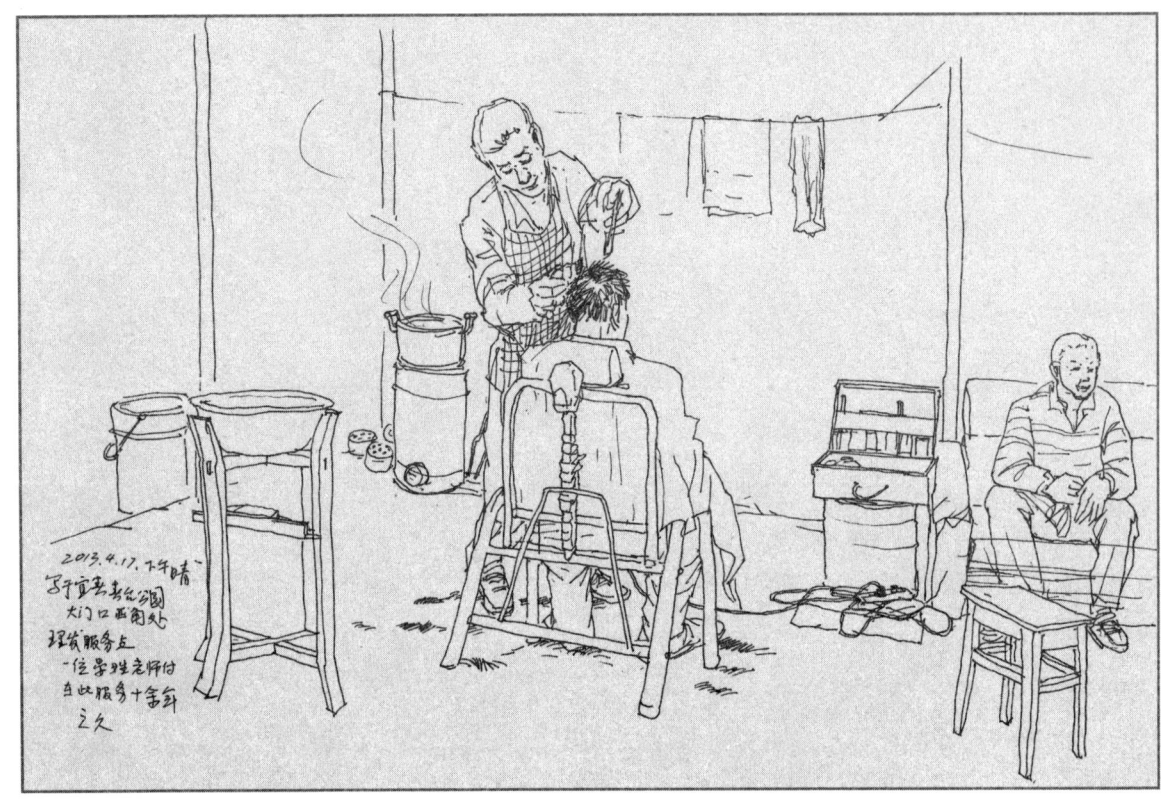

理发匠人

宜春公园一角有一便民理发点，服务热情，经济实惠，很受群众欢迎。据这位师傅说，他已在此为民服务了十年之久，风雨无阻。

Barber
There is a small barbershop in Yichun Park serving the locals. The barber provides customers warm service at reasonable prices, thus is quite popular. This barber said he had worked here for ten years, no matter rain or shine.

修理人力车

修车是一种脏活、累活，人们都生活在一个完整的链条式的社会中，每一个环节都很重要，缺一不可。故此，修车者也是生活中不可缺少的一分子。

Repairing Rickshaws

Repairing rickshaws is dirty, hard work, but indispensable for an inter-connected society. Rickshaw repairmen were indispensable in former days.

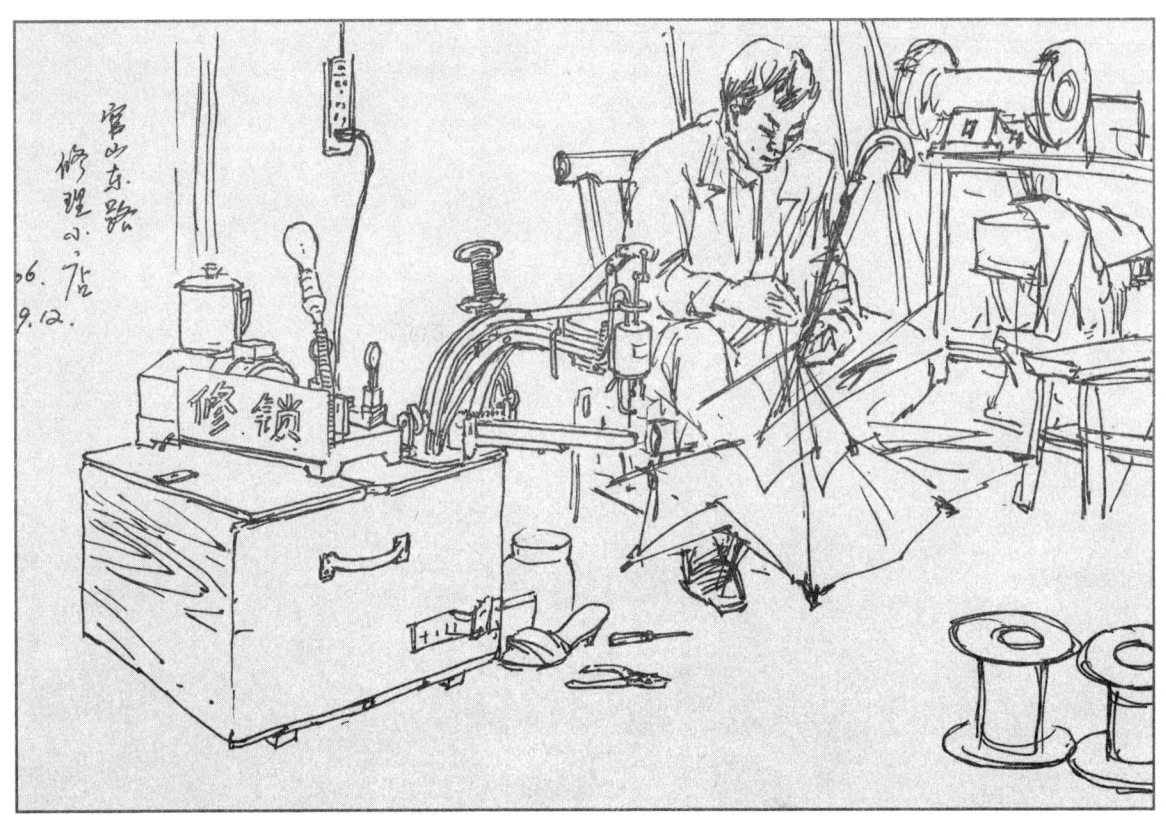

修伞者

修伞、修锁看似简单，其实手脚功夫里充满着智慧，不少发明家就是从拆件、安装、修理中起步的。

Craftsman Repairing Umbrellas
Repairing umbrellas, locks, etc. seem simple, but requires wits to successfully accomplish the details. Many inventors start with dismantling, installing and mending.

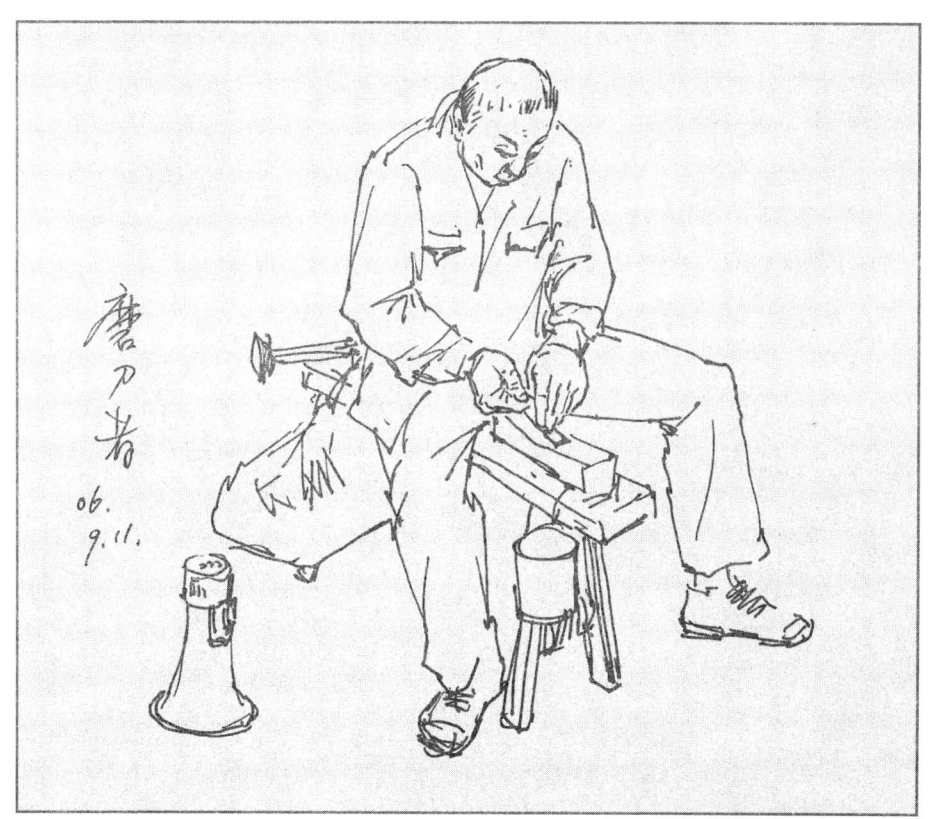

> 磨刀艺人

　　磨刀者越来越少，一是技难传，二是无人学，三是如今的刀具多为一次性产品，用完一丢买新的，不愿重复使用。

Craftsman Sharpening Knives

There are fewer and fewer knife sharpeners. The skill is difficult to learn; fewer people want to learn; knives are normally one-off tools, and many are not often used repeatedly.

工棚一角

　　城里的建设者队伍中,有来自不同地区的打工者,为了某一个工程他们吃苦耐劳,过着最低层生活。而往往这些建设者们是城市中不可缺少的,又是最容易被忘却的人。

A Bunkhouse Corner
Many construction workers in the city are migrants from other places. Though indispensable for the cities, they are often neglected.

| 鸭　苗 |

  春夏之交的季节是鸭苗上市的时期，金黄色的新鸭苗令人喜爱，小鸭的叫声也十分悦耳。宜春昔日西门菜市场是城内较大的市场，又是居民中心地段，物资十分丰富，整日热闹非常。

Ducklings
In late spring and early summer ducklings are available in market. They have a nice golden color and pleasantly quack.

127

屋前房后种瓜种豆

房前屋后种瓜种豆，在绿色环绕中生活，养鸡养鸭，自由自在心境特别安静，性情非常平和。

House Vegetable Gardens
Growing vegetables and raising poultry around the house has a calming effect.

城南郊外的菜地

宜春老火车站以南都算是城郊了，大片菜地郁郁葱葱，春意盎然。到菜地去散步，菜花香、泥土味扑面而来，坐在树荫底下写写生，心情特别愉快。

A Southern Suburb Vegetable Field

The areas south of the former railway station are divided into large plots of vegetables. I enjoyed walking in these fields or sitting and sketching under trees while enjoying the fragrance of flowers and soil.

滩下路的菜地

在西门滩下路的房屋群里发现一块绿色的菜地,心里感到很亲切,我顿时找个坐处,用速写记录下来。

Vegetable Field on Tanxia Road

I was touched when I encountered a vegetable field among the houses on Tanxia Road near the Western Gate. I decided to sit and sketch it at once.

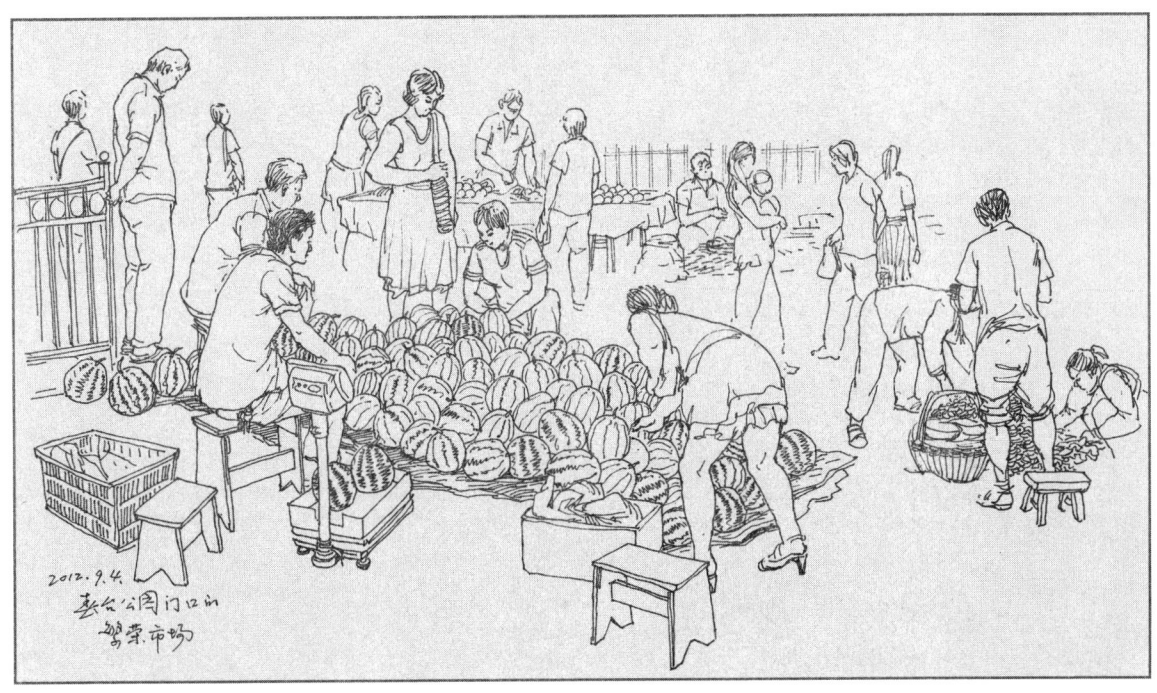

西瓜上市

　　小城市的优势也许就是离蔬果生产基地近得好。你看，刚刚从地里摘下的西瓜就上了市。这种新鲜口感大城市的居民是难以相比的。

Watermelons Ready for Sale

Being close to vegetable and fruit sources is one of the advantages of small cities. Impressively fresh watermelons are transported directly from the field to the market, a privilege seldom be enjoyed by big city residents.

油茶林场的农户

宜春油茶林场位于城南市郊，这里茂林沃土，花香鸟鸣，我时常会步行到林间菜地去写生。这家农户就住在林场的西侧，远离市区的繁华喧闹，安静舒适，悠闲自乐。

Farmers in a Camellia Farm

The Camellia Farm in the southern suburb of Yichun is a "sketching resort" with trees, wild flowers and singing birds. This family lives just west of the farm and enjoys a quiet and leisurely life here, far from the boisterous urban environment.

九旬老母亲

我九十岁的老母亲耳聪眼明,还可做一些力所能及的家务。母亲能高寿,这与她凡事心平气和有关。俗话说"家有一老,如获至宝"。

My Mother in Her 90s

Although in her 90s, my mother has good hearing and vision, and still helps with the housework. Her longevity is a result of her tranquility in dealing with daily affairs.

后 记

　　画速写是现场记实性的作画，绘画者多以此写生练笔、收集素材为目的。速写并非要求画得快，它不受任何形式、材料、时间和场合的约束，且时而会有可遇不可求的佳作出现。一张好的速写并不亚于所谓精雕细刻的创作。就绘画艺术而言，速写就是一个独立的画种。

　　画速写是我生活中不可缺少的一部分，是我主要的休闲方式，速写本随身带，走到那画到那，用自己的话说："我速写已上了瘾"。我在宜春生活了几十年，也用速写画了宜春几十年。随着时光的流逝，物移事迁，许多当年留下的速写作品已成为历史记忆中的画面。前不久，有两位宜春城南的老居民，特地登门从我速写本中复印了好几张作品，说是要带回去装框留作纪念。另有一位铜鼓县的朋友，将我速写本中的永宁老街等作品，用手机拍下后发到微信群中引来了热议，都感慨速写留住了岁月的记忆。

　　今年春季，我有幸结识了南昌大学来宜春挂职的毛静先生，在他的引见下，又认识了学苑出版社的洪文雄编辑，为此洪先生几次往返于北京，专程来我画室选作品，为我的速写出一本专辑，毛静先生还在百忙之中为书作序，这使我感激万分，几十年的速写耕耘若能为袁州记忆作出点绵薄之力，这的确是件值得欣慰的事。

严兴河
2015年秋于宜春介子堂